Counselling Parents
of Children
with Chronic Illness
or Disability

Hilton Davis

Communication and Counselling in Health Care
Series editor: Hilton Davis

Counselling Parents
of Children
with Chronic Illness
or Disability

Hilton Davis

Head of Child and Adolescent Psychology Services
Guys and Lewisham Trust

Medical advisor: Neil Marlow
Consultant Senior Lecturer in Paediatrics
University of Bristol

 Published by the British Psychological Society

First published in 1993 by BPS Books (The British Psychological Society),
St Andrews House, 48 Princess Road East, Leicester LE1 7DR.

Distributed exclusively in North America by Paul H. Brookes Publishing Co., Inc.,
P.O. Box 10624, Baltimore, Maryland 21285, U.S.A.

A catalogue record for this book is available from the British Library.

ISBN 1 85433 091 8 paperback
ISBN 1 85433 090 X hardback

Phototypeset by Gem Graphics, Trenance, Mawgan Porth, Cornwall
Printed in Great Britain by BPCC Wheatons Ltd, Exeter

OTHER TITLES IN THE SERIES
Counselling for Heart Disease by Paul Bennett

I should like to dedicate this book to my own family, Liz, Owen, Cara and Rachel, who have taught me so much about living, and to the families of children with chronic disease and disability who have shown me their strength and wisdom.

ACKNOWLEDGEMENTS

I am grateful to many people for their help in writing this book, especially the families who have allowed me to work with them. I have valued my contacts with the 0-2-5 Service in Essex, and the Avon Premature Infant Project. These groups have provided opportunities for intensive discussion about the issues raised in the book, and some of their members gave valuable feedback upon previous drafts. I am grateful to Neil Marlow for his very helpful comments and support, and for the help I have been given by the thoughtful members of the British Psychological Society Books and Special Projects Group. Rochelle Serwator must be congratulated for turning my words into readable English. I will ever be indebted to Prapti Ali Choudhury for her care, honesty, and humility, and for showing me what it really means to be a skilled helper. And, finally, I should like to thank my family for putting up with me throughout the writing process, and Liz for her special understanding.

CONTENTS

Foreword

This is an important book, not the least in its content but also, and more significantly, because of the readership that is its target. Communication skills have only recently arrived in medical school curricula, with differing degrees of emphasis and commitment, in parallel with changes in teaching programmes for allied professionals. The author has wide experience in helping medical and other professionals to unlock and demystify their relationships with patients, to move away from being an expert to being a partner in the patient's discovery and understanding. The importance of such skills in clinical practice cannot be understated and particularly when applied to helping parents whose children have a major disabling condition. The obvious clinical benefits, in terms of parental comprehension of the disease process, the accuracy of the diagnosis and amelioration of the family's stress and grief associated with chronic illness, seem often to have been ignored in the past.

Dr Davis sets out to present professionals with a reference framework and a basis for understanding and helping parents as they adapt to their child's problems. In doing this, he is often pointing out the obvious, but rarely considered, processes which occur naturally during an empathic counselling session. These processes need to be analysed and teased out to allow the professional to be of greater value to the family in situations where helping proves to be less straightforward.

Paediatricians are considered to need particularly sensitive communication skills, although postgraduate training is rare and career paths may self-select depending upon ability. Once in their final post, the concept that further personal development may occur is a foreign concept to many doctors. The recognition that such skills could be the subject of ongoing education would be a major advance, not just for the clinical professionals targeted by this book, but for all professionals working in the areas to be covered by the remaining volumes in this new series. I would hope that this volume will become the first of a series of standard texts and inspire teachers in their curriculum planning.

This volume has been written for a broad range of people comprising all helpers who come into contact with families who have children with chronic handicapping conditions – professionals and lay helpers, clinicians and non-clinicians. Therapists often hold beliefs that their practical intervention is the route by which change is wrought, without acknowledging their often considerable skills at less directive support. Few studies of the results of therapy have tried to separate out these effects: those that have, frequently show surprising results. Dr Davis and co-workers, through the East London Project, have demonstrated the positive value of non-directive support. I would strongly recommend the interested or doubting reader to look at this literature. How much more valuable would goal-directed intervention be if supported with helping and listening skills as described here?

Anyone who works with parents cannot fail to recognize the scenarios described in Dr Davis's clear and fascinating text as having parallels in their own practice. In reading many of the examples there is a feeling of *déjà vu*, but usually accompanied by a new panorama of the underlying dynamics. I have found this reference framework to be of tremendous value when dealing with the small, as well as the difficult problems, raised by parents, who are hungry for support but who desperately need to maintain their independence and self-respect, often in the face of conflicting 'expert' advice.

John Bunyan felt that Christian's progress was merely a vehicle for self-discovery and exhorted his reader to 'see if thou canst interpret it to me'. I hope that after reading this new volume, you will be encouraged to explore and discover aspects of everyday clinical interactions which help you to learn and improve your skills.

Neil Marlow
August 1992

Preface to the Series

People who suffer chronic disease or disability are confronted by problems that are as much psychological as physical, and involve all members of their family and the wider social network. Psychosocial adaptation is important in its own right, in terms of making necessary changes in life style, altering aspirations or coping with an uncertain future. However, it may also influence the effectiveness of the diagnostic and treatment processes, and hence eventual outcomes.

As a consequence, health care, whether preventive or treatment-oriented, must encompass the psychosocial integrated with the physical, at all phases of the life cycle and at all stages of disease. The basis of this is skilled communication and counselling by all involved in providing services, professionally or voluntarily. Everyone, from the student to the experienced practitioner, can benefit from appropriate training in this area, where the social skills required are complex and uncertain.

Although there is a sizeable research literature related to counselling and communication in the area of health care, specialist texts for training purposes are scarce. The current series was, therefore, conceived as a practical resource for all who work in health services. Each book is concerned with a specific area of health care. The authors have been asked to provide detailed information, from the patient's perspective, about the problems (physical, psychological and social) faced by patients and their families. Each book examines the role of counselling and communication in the process of helping people to come to terms and deal with these problems, and presents usable frameworks as a guide to the helping process. Detailed and practical descriptions of the major qualities, abilities and skills that are required to provide the most effective help for patients are included.

The intention is to stimulate professional and voluntary helpers alike to explore their efforts at supportive communication. It is hoped that by so doing, they become sufficiently aware of patient difficulties and the processes of adaptation, and more able to facilitate positive adjustment. The aims of the series will have been met if patients and families feel someone has listened and if they feel respected in their struggle for health. A central theme is the effort to make people feel better about themselves and able to face the future, no matter how bleak, with dignity.

Hilton Davis
Series editor

1

Setting the Scene

'*You will never forget the words. For as long as you live, through the sad times and the happy times, those words will always come back to you. Those first words the doctor spoke to you, telling you that there was a problem with your child. The way you accept and the way you begin to deal with the situation starts with those first words you hear.*'

(Krystyna Swirydczuk 1991, p.34)

Can you sense the hurt behind these words? The diagnosis of a chronic childhood disease or disability is a major crisis. It brings with it irreversible change. The world is instantly transformed in a nightmarish way. The sudden need to adapt to dreadful circumstances is forced upon the parents, their child, and indeed the whole family. Potentially they have to change their whole way of life, amid the terrible pain or anguish implied by the words above. Their vision of the world, their values, their ambitions, their whole philosophy will be altered by this one event.

The aims of this book are: 1) to explore this pain in order to understand the ways in which parents adapt to the diagnosis; and 2) on the basis of this understanding, to provide a practical model of the process of helping, and to describe the skills by which everyone working in the area of child health may facilitate the adaptation of the family. As a result, I hope the journey families are forced to undertake will become less lonely and traumatic, and more positive. The book is concerned with the provision of psychological and social help implemented simultaneously with physical care, but directed at the whole family. If carried out effectively, such care will not only improve the general well-being of the healthy members of the family, but will also have beneficial effects upon the physical treatment and psychological well-being of the child who is ill or disabled.

If you are working in any capacity, professionally or voluntarily, with children who are chronically ill or disabled, this book should have something to offer. Although service personnel do provide psychosocial care for their patients, commonly they do it from the heart, when and where they have the time, and when they feel comfortable and not overwhelmed by their own feelings, griefs and inadequacies. Such help is secondary to physical care, and systematic attention is rarely given to it. Health care personnel receive little training in the psychological frameworks and skills that are appropriate for effective all round help ing. Even if trained appropriately, professionals are rarely given the time or permission to use such skills properly for the benefit of the whole family.

I hope that what I say will provoke thought and stimulate solutions to problems confronted time and again. I am aware of the stress on people who work with children who cannot be cured. Feelings of personal inadequacy are constantly faced, and usually hidden. Such experiences are common to both parents and professionals, and may be less burdensome if shared. By thinking about the broader help ing processes, I hope that you will gain a greater appreciation of the value of listening. I would like you to feel more competent to listen to and respect the problems that families have, to accord them the dig nity of being able to cope, to make them proud of what they do, and to stand by them in their suffering. You might still feel the need to solve all the problems presented by families in their ordeal; but you cannot. No one can. Nor do you have to. You may not take away the pain, but your respectful presence may make the anguish more tolerable. If nothing else, you can make people feel good about them selves and therefore more competent and effective, no matter what the problem.

Whatever you gain from this book, I hope you retain a measure of self-doubt. This may be uncomfortable, particularly when you are called upon to help people in distress. However, humility is an essen tial ingredient of helping. It would be wonderful to be all-knowing, all-competent and confident, but, like everyone else, I am not. What comforts me, however, are the implications of my self-doubts:

- I have to respect the parents with whom I work.
- I must attribute to them the major role in dealing with the problems confronting them.
- I have to work *with* and *for* them, not *on* or *instead* of them.
- Above all, I have to listen.

We cannot take away chronic disease, but we can accept that the problems are real and they belong to the family. We can respect the family, in the knowledge that they will manage all their difficulties and more. We can also try to communicate our respect, because it may make them feel better about themselves and therefore more able to cope.

The wisdom of a young medical student struck me recently, when discussing how to inform parents of a terminal illness. He said, 'I could feel bad about hurting them, by giving them the news, and by not being able to do anything. On the other hand, by focusing my whole being on them, by making them, as people, the single reason for my training, I can do a lot'.

What Do I Mean by Counselling?

This book is to do with counselling, which is a word with multiple meanings and which, therefore, requires some attention. My definition is deliberately broad and refers to any situation in which there is mutual agreement that one person should interact with another in an attempt to help. The essence of this, therefore, is *helping*, but doing so by listening to and communicating with the person. This does not include acting for them or taking over from them; it does not simply involve giving them a drug or performing an operation on them. It does, however, include talking to them so that *they* can decide whether such actions are appropriate.

These comments on definition include a number of assumptions, which should be made explicit. These are:

- Respecting the individual's freedom to choose as they themselves see fit.
- Facilitation of the individual's own decision-making.
- Encouragement of the person's own effectiveness.
- Careful exploration of the situation/problem from the viewpoint of the person seeking help.
- Agreement of aims, and negotiation as necessary.
- Provision of relevant information, if possible, in ways that are clear and effective.

Counselling, therefore, as envisaged in this book, is not only about solving problems; it also has the more general intention of attempting to make people feel good about themselves. It equates to the term 'helping', as used by Egan (1982) in his problem management model, where the major concern is to provide the opportunity for people to help themselves.

Defined in this way, counselling can refer to a wide range of situations, potentially encompassing the work of all health care professionals who have patient contact. They are all trying to help, and if they acknowledge and use the basic skills of counselling, they may be more effective. Such skilled communication, if used appropriately at all stages of a disease, may not only facilitate optimum disease control but, at the very least, will not hinder psychological adaptation and, at best, may enhance it.

As an illustration, it can be said that the GP who simply gives a prescription to the patient is not counselling. This GP dominates the conversation, responds only to the patient's first complaint, does not explore the situation thoroughly and ends the consultation with a prescription. Not only is this not counselling, it is also poor practice. This is because the true nature of the complaint may not be communicated, so that the diagnosis may be incorrect, the treatment inappropriate and the outcome, therefore, inconclusive. Furthermore, the patient may not feel included in the process, may not be happy with the situation, may not trust the prescription and, as frequently happens, may not adhere to the treatment.

On the other hand, the GP is counselling if he/she provides the space in which patients can communicate the nature of the problem openly, explore it thoroughly and make explicit their worries and expectations before agreeing a set of aims to be pursued together. This physician is using the skills of facilitative communication, or basic counselling, which may result in more effective treatment, both physically and psychologically.

It is, however, necessary to distinguish between the work of health professionals generally and specialist counsellors. The latter are highly skilled professionals, whose training and aims focus on the many psychological and relationship problems that we all face in the course of our lives. At this level, the terms counselling, psychological therapy or psychotherapy are difficult to separate. The distinction, however, between health care professionals generally and specialist counsellors should not obscure the fact that, if they are effective, they will both use the same basic counselling skills, and will have aims in common. At the specialist level, however, there are additional elements. These include: a more formal relationship; explicit concern for psychological and social issues; a wider range of skills and techniques; broader theory relating to psychological and social functioning and the processes of change; and, finally, more extensive training.

Help for Whom?

What I have to say derives from extensive clinical involvement with families of children with problems of all kinds. My concerns here, however, are specifically with families of children who have a chronic disease or disability. The ideas are applicable whatever the composition of the family (for example, nuclear or extended, single or two parents) and regardless of the nature or severity of the disease or disability. This, therefore, potentially involves something like 18% of children, according to estimates derived from population surveys like the Ontario Child Health Study (Cadman, *et al.*, 1987).

Some of these children and their families, to be found in all health care facilities, are so extremely distressed that they are a major concern to the professionals caring for them. My aim in this book is to enable professionals to help these families more effectively. However, much more important in my opinion, is to prevent this level of distress from occurring in the first place. My major concern, therefore, is that *all* professionals might find something of value in this book to help them support *all* families at *all* stages of the illness in ways that enable them to avoid as much distress as possible.

I will use the words, disease or illness, to refer to an ongoing problem of the physical functioning of the body described in relation to a pattern of signs and symptoms, their expected development, and the underlying pathology and causes. The term, disability, is defined more behaviourally, to refer to what the child is prevented from doing as a result of disease or injury. All illnesses can have such effects, although some will be more significant than others.

By definition, most of the conditions considered here cannot be cured. Once acquired, as the result of injury, infection, or genetic defect, they last for years, sometimes for life. Treatment is, therefore, at best palliative and symptomatic. It may be of only limited benefit, and it may bring side-effects, usually limited to the duration of the treatment. These effects, however, may be permanent and disastrous, as in the case of children with haemophilia treated with blood products contaminated with HIV.

By far the most common diseases are eczema, which occurs in about 8% to 10% of children, and asthma, with estimates in the region of 2% to 5%. Diabetes is relatively common, occurring in about 1.8% of children. Congenital heart disease, mostly diagnosed in the first year of life, has an estimated prevalence of 0.2% to 0.7% of children. Other common diseases include the various forms of epilepsy (0.26% to 0.46%), cerebral palsy (0.14% to 0.5%), other brain injuries (about 0.2%), cleft lip and palate (0.13% to 0.2%), Down's syndrome (about 0.1%), and juvenile rheumatoid arthritis (0.1% to 0.3%). Somewhat less common, but no less serious, are sickle cell disease (about 0.046%), autism (about 0.04%), spina bifida (about 0.04%), cystic fibrosis (0.02%), haemophilia (0.015%), phenylketonuria (0.01%), kidney disease (0.008%), and muscular dystrophy (0.006%). Although leukaemia (0.01%) and other cancers are not necessarily chronic, in that many are now cured, they will be included as they are life-threatening, the treatment may be extended over long periods and the threat of recurrence is ever present.

Disability may result from any of these identifiable conditions, as well as from injuries and, as yet, unknown causes. The most common are intellectual disability in 2% to 3% of children, visual impairment in 2% to 3.5%, and hearing impairment in about 1.6%. Motor difficulties in locomotion and/or manipulation are a frequent accompaniment to all disease and injury.

The well-being of the child is central to the aims of this book. However, my thesis is that this is best achieved by a policy of care for the whole family, mediated via the parents. The focus of this book is, therefore, upon the professional–parent relationship rather than the direct relationship between the professional and child. The psychosocial adaptation of parents should be of central concern to every professional, because of the crucial role of the parents in all aspects of the care and treatment of the child. The concerns of parents have often been neglected by professionals in their concerns for the diseases of children, yet it is the parents who take responsibility for and carry out most of the treatment of the child, both physically and psychologically. Therefore, although professionals do treat children directly, for the most part it is only through the parents that they have access, legally, practically and morally, to the child. Relatively little can be done without the cooperation of parents, unless, of course, one removes the child from their care, as is legally possible in the con-text, for example, of child abuse. If parents do not agree with the professional, do not have appropriate information, or their adaptation is otherwise compromised by the stresses upon them, they will be unlikely or unable to do what professionals advise. As a result, the effectiveness of any treatment for the child will be severely limited.

I will not, therefore, focus on the skills of counselling children directly, as this would take a book in its own right. My assumption is that, as a professional, one should do all one can to help the parents themselves to communicate effectively with their children, so as to help them cope with the ravages of disease and, for example, to prepare them for painful treatment procedures. This is not to under-estimate the importance of professional–child communication, as professionals must also be skilled at communicating directly with children in all contacts with them. However, it is important to realize that the principles and skills of doing so are essentially the same as those for communicating with parents, and these are described in detail in this book.

Who are the Helpers?

The content of this book is relevant to all people working in the area of paediatrics. This includes medical staff (from the consultant to the house officer), nurses, physiotherapists, speech therapists, radiographers, social workers and teachers. Other ward staff, such as receptionists and auxiliaries, may also find it useful, as will people in the community, from GPs to community nurses and health visitors. These, and others, including volunteers, have a role to play in providing counselling support. All of them can play a role in helping families, supporting them and making them feel better about themselves.

There is evidence that the use of appropriate counselling skills may result in a number of improvements. Davis and Fallowfield (1991a) discuss the following benefits: greater satisfaction and less stress for professionals; greater patient satisfaction; improved diagnostic validity; increased patient knowledge; improved adherence to treatment regimes; less psychosocial distress; improved physical response to treatment; and a greater likelihood of prevention. The argument is that if all people working in the services were to incorporate the knowledge and skills of basic counselling into their everyday work with families of children with chronic disease, then there would be enormous benefits for all concerned (professionals, parents and children).

Although individuals working in isolation may make such improvements, it is my contention that the benefits would be far greater if their work was organized and coordinated. This should begin with agreed policy about the provision of general psychosocial support for families as a whole. These broader organizational issues will be addressed in the final chapter of the book. However, the ideal I have in mind derives from my work in setting up the Parent Adviser Scheme (Davis and Rushton, 1991) where counselling support was provided on a long-term basis for families of children with multiple disabilities. Relatively brief systematic training in basic counselling skills was given to both professionals (for example, health visitors and physiotherapists) and non-professionals, who were then allocated a small number of families to visit regularly, over extended periods. Each was to act as a keyworker for these families, with the intention of establishing a mutually respectful relationship with the family, to help them explore the problems confronting them, and to help them decide appropriate aims and strategies. Experimental evaluation of the intervention found it to be effective both in facilitating the general adaptation of parents and in improving the developmental progress and behaviour of their children.

Because this book is concerned with basic counselling skills as applied to the role of all people working in the area of paediatrics, the convention will be to use the term *helper* to refer to them all. This is convenient in that it encompasses every diverse profession involved, without having to be specific. The term *professional* is an alternative, but is less useful in that it does not refer to people who are not professionally trained and who may act, for example, as volunteers, either in the health service or in a voluntary organization. I will not use the term *counsellor* to apply to those using basic skills, as the use of these skills will, in general, be an adjunct to the pursuit of a person's own professional expertise, such as medicine or nursing. Instead, *counsellor* will be reserved for those with extensive training in the high level skills necessary to undertake the provision of psychological help as their primary role.

The Plan of the Book

To help parents adapt to the difficulties they face, it is appropriate to begin by listening to them. This is, in fact, a major help in itself, and involves providing parents with the circumstances in which they feel able to express their concerns, as well as listening to them carefully while they talk. It is therefore appropriate to begin the book with the parents, and to give some indication of the problems they face, and how they adapt to and cope with their child's illness. In the next chapter, therefore, I will outline a framework for understanding the processes by which parents adapt to the crises of paediatric illness – illustrating the difficulties they experience and the changes they have to make. Every person is unique in their adaptation, which is the result of an interplay between the models they have for understanding their world prior to the illness, and the disruption caused by the trauma. In Chapter 3, I will consider the aims of helping parents to adapt, before discussing a partnership model of the helper–parent relationship, and providing an overall model of the helping process to serve as a guide.

Chapters 4, 5 and 6 will be concerned with describing in detail the fundamental qualities and attitudes required in helpers. These chapters will explain the specific skills needed at each stage of the helping process, beginning with the first meeting and the initiation of the relationship with the parents. Careful attention will be given to the breaking of bad news which, if done well, provides the means of establishing a model of ongoing long-term help. The book concludes with a consideration of some remaining questions relating to the training of the helper, supervision and support, and other organizational issues to do with the system in which help is to be provided. This will include looking at the referral of the family for specialist psychological help and the evaluation of effectiveness.

I hope that you enjoy the book, and that it inspires you to think carefully and creatively about how you can interact with parents more effectively. You will probably have achieved this if parents are able to say about you what one mother said about her paediatrician:

'She was a great doctor; she really knew what she was doing with our daughter. But she also knew what she was doing with us. She always listened to what we had to say. She treated us like adults, made us feel involved. She told us what was going on. She made us feel important, and that we could manage. We came away feeling we could make decisions for ourselves and do things.'

2

Family Adaptation to Disease

Linda was sitting in the car next to her husband, tired but relaxed from the lovely day at the seaside. She was enjoying the evening sunshine as they stopped at traffic-lights on their way home. Suddenly she heard the screech of tyres, and then a loud bang as she was violently thrown forward but restrained by her seat-belt. Another car had run into the back of them. The thought of how lucky they were to have such a strong car and belts for the children ran quickly through her mind, as she asked if everyone was all right. Looking round she saw only two of her children, and then froze as she saw her seven-year-old daughter slumped on the floor with her head covered in blood. She had not been wearing her seat-belt and had severely damaged her skull as she hit the doorpost.

This tragic event was a transition point for the family, the beginning of a nightmare. The child lived, although it was a tenuous existence for several horrifying weeks. During this time, the parents sat by her bedside or anxiously awaited her return from theatre, where the surgeons attempted to repair the massive injury. Home life stopped for this family for several months, and the other children were left with whoever could look after them. The parents had little time for them. When they were at home they were preoccupied; father drank heavily, mother was irritable.

The family rejoiced when the child was eventually discharged from hospital; they believed their worries were nearing an end. It took many months, however, for them to realize they had lost their bright, beautiful, sunny child forever. In her place was a badly disfigured girl who could hardly walk, had only a few words of speech and screamed frequently. The family struggled for some time, attending all their appointments at the distant hospital with the paediatrician, the occupational therapist and the physiotherapist. They were subjected to the harrowing experience of the educational statementing procedure, designed to provide access to special education. Family life ceased to exist. The other children began to be unhappy and to do badly at school. The parents lost their friends. They became more and more disillusioned and depressed. Although they did what the professionals said, little progress occurred. They began to argue with the professionals and failed to keep appointments. As a result they were labelled as difficult.

By chance, however, they began to see a health visitor attached to their local health centre, and she spent time with them at home and in the surgery over a period of weeks. She listened to them carefully and helped them to explore what was happening to them. She did not try to take their problems away, but helped them to list each of their worries, to clarify the problem and to think of ways to adapt. Most important from their viewpoint, she valued them, and very slowly they responded. The child was not cured, but the other members of the family began to feel better and began to function as a unit. They had direction and purpose. The parents still worked with professionals, but they became much more self-reliant, questioned what was prescribed and made final decisions for themselves.

When children are hurt, ill or disabled, they need physical and personal attention, and this has consequences for all members of the family. At a relatively trivial level, one of the parents has to stop cooking, reading or watching television to see to the child, to cuddle him/her or kiss a bruise better. If the child is sick, parents become worried, arrangements have to be made to look after her/him while one parent takes the other children to school, or they have to make time to go to the GP. Time may be lost from work, and the other children lose attention. Such consequences are a routine part of family life but, in chronic disease, they become a way of life. Anxiety may be the norm, outside commitments may be impossible and childcare duties are increased, including appointments with professionals and even periods away from home for hospital admissions.

Each disease presents specific problems to the child and family. Such problems vary according to the nature, frequency, visibility and severity of symptoms, the degree to which they are disabling or life-threatening, and the demands of the necessary treatment. Each condition has specific stresses and makes particular demands upon the resources of the child and family. Common to them all, however, is the need to adapt physically, psychologically and socially. This is as true for diabetes or eczema, as for leukaemia, galactosaemia, visual impairment or sickle cell anaemia. Children and their parents have to change and adapt to a set of undesirable and unfortunate circumstances, and the processes of adaptation are as similar between conditions as within. Indeed, it can be argued, that even within a specific disease category, the problems confronted by a family are more to do with characteristics of the people than of the disease itself.

Therefore, to work successfully with families, to communicate with them helpfully, not only involves knowledge of particular diseases, but also knowledge of the family. This can only be gained by listening to the family members carefully, in a dialogue that facilitates open communication. Since paediatric services rarely address these issues directly and systematically, many of us have little knowledge of the adjustments that are required in the struggle to cope. To help parents and children as people, requires a clear understanding of the problems they face, the sense they make of events, and the ways they adapt. I will, therefore, begin by considering the general effects of disease and disability, as indicated by research studies, before describing a framework to help make sense of the processes of adaptation, and to illustrate in detail the kinds of problems parents and their children face. Although I will frequently use the word 'parents' in the plural throughout the book, this is meant to indicate parents in general, and not to imply that there is always more than one parent in a particular family.

Effects of Disease and Disability

Research studies in the area of paediatrics indicate high levels of psychological and social disturbance. Children who are ill are twice as likely to have psychological disorders (behaviour problems and emotional difficulties) as healthy children (Cadman *et al.*, 1987), and such difficulties may outlast the disease by many years, as in the case of children who have recovered from cancer. The rate of disturbance is about 20% to 25% as opposed to 10% to 15% in the healthy. If the child is also disabled, the rate of disturbance rises to between 30% and 35%. Cognitive and academic functioning may also be affected as a direct result of disease and the toxicity of treatment, and because of distress, behaviour problems, missed schooling and other family difficulties.

Parents are, of course, profoundly affected by illness in their children, with as many as 33% of parents of children with cancer, even in remission, having such severe depression and anxiety that they require professional help (Hughes and Lieberman, 1990). In a recently completed study with one of my students, 31% of mothers of children with diabetes were found to have stress levels that would have benefited from professional mental health intervention.

Communication and relationship problems are also common, reflected in increased marital distress, if not in divorce (Sabbeth and Leventhal, 1984). This suggests that families may not function so well as a unit where there is chronic disease and disability. There is evidence of increased disturbance in siblings, including irritability, social withdrawal, jealousy and guilt, academic under-achievement, behaviour problems, anxiety, and low self-esteem. A major theme appears to be the disruption of their social relationships, especially with their parents, and feeling neglected in comparison with the child who is ill.

Eiser (1990) and Garrison and McQuiston (1989) provide comprehensive reviews of the research findings cited above. Such results focus upon the negative and the extreme, and it must be acknowledged that there is considerable variation in the degree to which families adapt. Although all family members experience considerable stress and distress at various times in the course of the child's illness, there is a range of reactions from those who adapt extremely well to those who collapse. The level of adaptation and the ways in which people cope are important concerns in themselves, but they also affect the course of the illness and the extent to which it is treated effectively. For both reasons, therefore, it is important to understand the processes of adaptation so that we may be able to predict those most at risk.

However, the processes involved in adaptation are not well understood. It is, therefore, difficult to predict the level of adaptation for an individual family, their methods of coping, or the factors that contribute to the process. Models have been proposed (for example, Wallander *et al.*, 1989) that consider the interaction between risk factors and resistance factors. Risk factors include, for example, the characteristics of the disease, the demands made upon care-taking, and associated and/or unrelated stressors. Resistance factors involve all the individual, interpersonal and more general ecological resources that enable people to cope. Such factors are assumed to be interrelated and to have both direct and indirect effects upon adaptation in physical, social and emotional terms.

Although such models may be useful, actual research has been limited, so that conclusions remain tentative and incomplete. Pless and Nolan (1991) provide the most recent review of factors predicting adaptation in children specifically, with Eiser (1990) and Garrison and McQuiston (1989) looking at the family as a whole. The results suggest that:

> Disease category does not clearly predict adaptation, although children with brain dysfunction, disability or sensory impairment have a greater incidence of psychosocial problems.
> Severity of disease as assessed by parents (not professionals) is associated with poorer adaptation.
> As the degree of debilitation and pain increase, there is an associated increase in psychological difficulty.

➤ Diseases with a high probability of fatality are associated with greater levels of psychological disorder, both in children and their parents.

➤ The visibility of disease appears to predict good child adaptation. Perhaps this is because the difficulties are self-evident to the onlooker, therefore creating fewer problems for parents and children in relation to the people around them.

➤ Socioeconomic status is not consistently related to the level of adaptation of either the child or the parents.

➤ The gender of the child is not associated with adjustment.

➤ Psychological problems in children appear to increase as children get older, with adolescence as a particularly troublesome time.

➤ Family variables such as open, honest communication, lack of conflict, family cohesion, emotional expressiveness and family stability are predictive of the ability of the child and parents to cope with the disease and disease control.

➤ Family size, marital status, and ethnicity do not appear to predict child or parental adjustment.

➤ Parental depression and ill health increase the risk of problems with the child.

➤ Concurrent stresses, both within and outside the family, are predictive of outcome in maternal and child adaptation.

➤ Previous severe psychological problems in the parents are associated with difficulties in adapting to disease.

➤ There is some evidence that increasing parental age is related to greater adaptation.

➤ Social or emotional support, including marital satisfaction, are related to level of parent and child adaptation.

Understanding Adaptation: a Framework

Although these research findings are important and potentially useful in many ways, they do not tell us much about specific families. The provision of effective help for parents, and hence for the family as a whole, requires an understanding of individual parents, the ways they interact, the ways they adapt to the experience of chronic illness and the kinds of problems they encounter in the process. I will, therefore, outline a framework for making sense of the psychological processes by which individual parents experience new and distressing events, and adapt to them. At the same time, I will attempt to illustrate many of the problems and issues that they have to face in the continuing crisis of chronic disease and disability.

What I have to say owes much to the work of George Kelly, a psychologist, who devised the theory of personal constructs. Comprehensive descriptions of this theory can be found, for example, in Kelly (1991) and Bannister and Fransella (1986).

For the purpose of understanding parental adaptation, I am going to assume that each person, adult or child, is like a scientist, in the sense that we are constantly in the process of constructing, in our head, a theory or model about our world in order to anticipate what is going to happen to us. The importance of anticipation is that it allows us to adapt efficiently, as opposed to living in a constant state of anxiety in which we never know what is going to happen. Each person constructs a model that is unique, based upon their individual experience. It is the uniqueness of each model that explains the fact that people react so differently to events. The assumption is, therefore, that it is not the event that determines our reactions and feelings, but our individual interpretations (or *constructions*) of the event.

Although the individual's model, or *construct system*, is reasonably stable, it is nevertheless being tested against the stream of ongoing experience. As with a scientist, each of our anticipations is a kind of hypothesis, and our action related to each anticipation is a type of experiment, which serves to validate or refute the hypothesis depending upon the outcome. For example, a mother who construed her son as incredibly strong and brave in tolerating the constant need to take blood samples, was shocked when he suddenly screamed and fought, and refused to cooperate in the procedure. Her hypothesis concerning this aspect of her child's behaviour had to be revised dramatically. She had to rethink what was happening to him, and to think of other ways of helping him to cope.

As we shall see, the process of helping parents is one of exploring with them the hypotheses they have about their world so as to clarify and, if necessary, change them. The ways of doing this are primarily through discussion and listening, but there are a variety of possible methods. To illustrate the model that a parent may have about his/her child, I would like to describe what may be called a child characterization sketch. One might, however, use similar methods to elucidate any aspect of the parent's construct system.

The parent is simply asked to describe his/her child (the child's behaviour or personality) in as much detail as possible, and what is said is recorded verbatim. This can be done by asking parents to write the sketch, or alternatively by using a cassette recorder as they speak. The following came from a father whose major concern was his daughter's failure to be reliable in giving herself insulin injections:

> *'She is being extremely difficult. She used to be so compliant. She would do*
> *everything she was told. We had such a good relationship. Now . . . well! She*
> *seems to be provoking me. I try to be a good father, and I'm concerned about her*
> *diabetes, but if I mention anything to do with her injections, she goes out of her*
> *way to do something to upset me. If I ask her whether she has taken her*
> *insulin, she says "I can't remember." . . . Whenever I say anything to her she*
> *screams at me.'*

This passage begins to provide a picture of the constructs this father uses to anticipate his teenage daughter. It reflects the unique model that he has constructed from his experiences with her, although it may or, in this case, may not correspond to the model constructed by others such as his daughter or his wife. His daughter, for example, disagreed with him completely; she saw herself as taking care of her diabetes reasonably well, but she saw her father not as 'good' or 'concerned', but as interfering and 'never interested in me, just my disease'.

The father's overall model or construct system is made up of a number of specific constructs, such as 'she is extremely difficult' or 'provoking' or 'goes out of her way . . . to upset me'. Each of these is a specific construct by which he anticipates or predicts her behaviour. These are the aspects of his daughter that are noticeable or have significance for him. Each is not an isolated observation, but is related to all his other constructs to form an organized model or system, in which some constructs will be more important (*superordinate*) than others in that they have more implications. What is also clear, is that the way he construes himself is highly related to his constructions of his daughter, as in his construction of himself as 'trying to be a good father'.

Perhaps what is most important to realize in considering this example of an individual model, is that what the person sees is not necessarily a direct reflection of reality. It is that person's reality, and the business of helping is to discover the person's existing constructions, to help them test these, and to help them gain a more useful model enabling more accurate predictions. On this basis, the individual parent will be better equipped to adapt to whatever circumstances surround them. One should be careful to note, however, that the example above tells us only about the constructions this father put into words. There may be many that he uses that he did not mention, is not able to put into words, or may not even realize. In fact, much of what this book is about, is the process of enabling parents to talk freely, to explore their constructions, to see the ways in which constructs relate to one another, and possibly to become conscious of constructs they use without awareness. One might, for example, infer that this father does not realize the extent to which he is confusing his constructions of the illness with his constructions of his daughter.

The Crisis of Diagnosis

The model a parent uses to make sense of her/his life evolves slowly for the most part. How they see their children and themselves as parents may change somewhat rapidly at some points, like at the birth of the child, but otherwise probably changes relatively slowly as the child develops. At the point of diagnosis of a serious disease, however, a major and sudden change is dramatically precipitated. This is a serious crisis, a point at which rapid and significant change has to occur in the parent's model and behaviour.

At the disclosure of the diagnosis, parents often describe a state of shock, numbness or confusion. They talk about not being able to understand what is being said. They describe a turmoil of questions, images and ideas in their heads.

'And so it went on, thoughts scrambling around like rats in a cage, all night long.'　　　　　　　　　　　　　　　　　　　　(Byard 1991, p.47)

'I heard him say there was a need for an operation, but I didn't hear anything else. I had no idea what he was saying.'

This represents a state of extreme anxiety. Parents are aware that the events with which they are suddenly confronted lie beyond the range of their constructs. Their existing construct system, the way in which they anticipate the world, is suddenly irrelevant, or rather its relevance is uncertain as the world has suddenly changed. The turmoil is a temporary state in which they are unable to understand what is happening. They are not able to make immediate or long-term predictions about anything, since they do not have instant access to a model of this new world.

The process of adaptation starts immediately, but the discovery of the illness is only the beginning. It is a process in which the parents have to change their constructions to accommodate new and unforeseen events. These may unfold step by step, or may occur dramatically and suddenly. The process is not fast, because the changes in the construct system are likely to be profound and widespread, and events often unfold unevenly with, for example, the development of a new symptom or the need for more surgery. Uncertainty will arise at each new stage of the illness, and parents will have to change each time. For example, they will accommodate first to the child having heart disease, and then to the need for surgery. They may then have to come to terms with the wait for an operation, even though the child's life is at risk, and at some point have to deal with disconcerting information (such as the risk of death in open heart surgery is 12% to 18%).

The pre-diagnostic construct system still exists after the initial shock, and may guide the process of adaptation during which the parent's model is rebuilt. This is very much a process of hypothesis testing and experimentation, as mentioned earlier, and has to be based upon what the parents already know. They try to make sense of the illness with reference to what they used to think. For example, one woman explored carefully what her child had eaten, whether she was simply tired, and whether there was a virus about. This was how she had always understood illness. She retained for some time a model of illness as trivial and short-term, even though the child had leukaemia. She may have been accused of denial, but she was actually retaining original constructs in order to maintain some understanding and to test her hypotheses.

At another extreme, a mother who had apparently always been frightened of her child dying, believed that her child was very close to death after the diagnosis of diabetes. She was using pre-existing constructs and did not have the opportunity to test them properly as she simply was labelled as neurotic and not given a proper hearing by the medical or nursing staff.

Specific Areas of Change and Problems

To illustrate the changes and the problems faced in adapting to the diagnosis, I will look at different aspects of the construct system. The intention is to show the diversity of constructions and changes, and the range of problems and issues. The points made will not relate to all parents, since each is unique and has a construct system that is peculiar to them, both in content and organization. This massive variation can be explored simply by talking to parents about themselves and their families, and by reading what they have to say about their experiences (for example, Cooper and Harpin, 1991). At a general level, however, there will be some similarity in that each parent will have subsystems of constructs, even before the diagnosis, concerned with, for example: each of their children, their spouse/partner, the extended family, friends and neighbours, all aspects of daily life (house, car, money, etc.), and their general philosophy of life. We shall explore each of these subsystems in turn, but we will begin with the most obvious area of change, the parents' constructions of illness. Usually parents will have very few constructions of illness at the point of diagnosis, and it is here that enormous change has to occur very quickly.

Constructions of the illness

Being told that their child has a chronic disease (for example, leukaemia or spina bifida) will have little meaning for most parents initially. They face a state of uncertainty, varying from complete ignorance ('I had simply never heard of Fallot's tetralogy'), to some limited knowledge ('I had given money for leukaemia, but I didn't really know what it was'). They therefore experience high anxiety, not to say horror. Even if the parent has extensive knowledge of a disease, there is still vast uncertainty inherent in most diagnoses in that all diseases are variable in their course, and therefore specific prediction is difficult.

Given the lack of constructs at this point, it is not surprising that, initially, the worst possible picture may be seen. This is because it is easier to anticipate what is to be lost. Certainly, anticipations may be extreme in many instances, either overly optimistic or pessimistic. Parents frequently begin from a point of misinformation or misconstruction, assuming, for example, either that all tumours can simply be removed, or that they spell automatic death. One family understandably thought the word 'malignant' was used to refer to their child being evil, as opposed to referring to a cancer.

The process of building a construct system about the disease begins immediately, although it may remain problematic for years after the diagnosis. Parents start to acquire information about the symptoms of the disease, the causes, the prognosis and treatment, including the skills they need to carry out necessary testing and treatments (for example, application of creams, use of inhalers, injections or urine testing). The acquisition process varies enormously, however, from parent to parent because of differences in learning ability, understanding, prior knowledge, access to information and other personal characteristics. Some parents, for example, will want to know every detail, no matter how dreadful, whereas others wish to know little. Some want to be very certain about the future, whereas others simply take each day as it comes: 'I live for today. I want to know nothing about tomorrow, let alone next year'. For these reasons, the progression of an illness may come as a devastating surprise (for example, the development of bladder, kidney and intellectual difficulties in spina bifida). On the other hand, it may be no surprise at all, as in the case of a mother who could not stop herself from worrying about further deterioration in her son's disease, even though the possibility of this occurring was remote.

The parents' acquisition of an adequate understanding of the disease is an ongoing problem. One mother, who had never in seven years had an adequate diagnosis for her son's relatively mild neuromuscular difficulties, suddenly told of her worries (that she need not have had) that her child had either motor neurone disease or multiple sclerosis. Such problems arise for several reasons:

- Professionals frequently provide too little information, or do not provide it at the correct time and in an appropriate way.
- Parents may have limited access to information from other sources (for example, reading material) especially if their first language is not English or they are poorly educated and/or under-privileged.
- Friends and acquaintances may provide information that is inaccurate and often conflicting.
- The disease process may unfold very slowly.
- The course and the prognosis may be unpredictable.

Particular problems arise where the cause of a disease is not known as, for example, in unspecified developmental delay. However, this may be alleviated to some extent if the syndrome has a name (for example, autism or Noonan's syndrome).

A major issue is, of course, the extent to which the disease can be treated, ameliorated or kept at bay. Where little can be done, parents face the task of coming to terms with this fact. The process will vary from parent to parent, relating to other aspects of their construct system, such as their self-concept. For some, the diagnosis will be yet another sign of their lifelong inability to influence whatever happens to them. For others, this will be the first time they have ever experienced something that they have not been able to control. Most parents will, not unnaturally, test the hypothesis that the paediatrician is wrong. Many will do this simply by thinking about it, or discussing it with those close to them. Some parents will do it by asking for a second opinion. Some will explore alternative medicine. A few parents, however, will embark upon a desperate and, sadly, fruitless search for further information and expertise – nationally, or even internationally, shopping around for a cure. A good relationship between the professional and the parent may make this unnecessary.

A frequent issue for parents is the evaluation of the relative costs (physical, financial, emotional) and benefits of the treatment available for their child. This is particularly obvious where the child is subjected to investigations and treatments that are in themselves painful (for example, lumbar punctures and bone marrow aspirations), distressing (for example, chemotherapy) or dangerous as in some surgical procedures (for example, for heart disease). Parents are constantly in the frightening situation of deciding what to do, balancing the known harm of the treatment with frequently unknown benefits. Despite subjecting the child to the pain and nausea of chemotherapy, with side-effects such as hair loss and lethargy, their child may still die, and they will live with the consequences of their decision for many years. Whether to accept heart surgery with a high risk of death or to refuse and thereby reduce the child's life span, is an unenviable decision. Factors like the length of stay in hospital, its accessibility and the quality of the relationship with the staff may be influential here.

Even where a procedure carries a known probability of outcome, as in surgery or chemotherapy, there is the problem of knowing what this means to individual parents. The outcome of most developmental therapies has never been adequately assessed, and therefore parents have to decide whether to spend time (for example, from one to several hours per day) stimulating, teaching or exercising their child with Down's syndrome or cerebral palsy with little knowledge of the likely benefits. The decision to carry out such intensive programmes (from Portage to conductive education) must take circumstances other than outcome into account. Such issues need careful discussion with parents, so that those who are desperate to try anything to help their child may do so realistically, and those who feel generally burdened may not be made to feel guilty.

Parental commitment to treatment is a crucial issue. It must be addressed by all those purporting to provide help for children with chronic disease. Parents will quickly tire of regimented or unrealistic treatment regimes, from the constant application of creams in skin diseases to dietary restrictions, without evidence of benefit. There will always be other distractions and pressures on them, such as their own tiredness, the child's reluctance and other life demands. These, coupled with fears about the long-term effects and side-effects of the treatments, can easily persuade parents not to comply with instructions.

Constructions of professionals

As they develop constructs about the disease, parents also have to build a set of constructs about the professionals who care for their child. They may never have heard of a dietician or an oncologist. Parents have to discover what various professionals do and what they expect if they are to work effectively together. This includes getting to know, respect and trust them. Ideally, if they construe professionals as helpful, understanding, trustworthy, supportive and respectful, then the parents' ability to cope with the disease and treatment is likely to be enhanced, or at least not hindered.

Unfortunately, parents suggest that systematic professional concern for the parent–professional relationship is neglected. Research studies indicate that professional communication is by far the greatest source of consumer complaint, and observational studies indicate the need for considerable improvements (see Davis and Fallowfield, 1991b). Although communication can be extremely good, there have been studies indicating rates of dissatisfaction as high as 70% in mothers of children with a variety of illnesses. Published surveys suggest that only about 50% of parents are satisfied with the ways in which they are initially informed of the diagnosis.

Complaints include not being told immediately, together and in private. Parents also complain of not being informed sympathetically, in words they understand, and with enough time being allocated. Consideration is frequently not given to the complexity of parents' feelings as they experience the shock of the disclosure. Recent unpublished research suggests that follow-up appointments are now more common than they were although parents may wait for much longer than a week.

Parents ask to be treated respectfully, 'as intelligent human beings, as adults, and not children'. They want professionals to listen to them, and to acknowledge their own expertise as parents. They request the sharing of information and negotiation so that they are involved in decision-making. They value honesty and encouragement, and they ask that their child be treated with respect as an individual, and that the family as a whole be considered, not just the disease.

> *'Probably the most important thing that my paediatrician did in those important early days was to place such heavy emphasis on Natalia as a child first and foremost, rather than focusing on the fact that my child belonged to a population of people who were born with an extra chromosome.'*
>
> (Swirydczuk 1991, p.39)

Given that parental adaptation is of prime importance to the whole task of dealing with the child's illness or disability, poor professional communication will not help and may even make it more difficult. Mothers frequently feel that staff see them as 'demanding', 'neurotic' or 'over-anxious', especially prior to diagnosis when they feel something is wrong, but no one listens. If parents are to develop completely new constructions, professionals need to provide first class information, they need to be extremely competent at communicating, and should be construed as credible, as opposed to uncaring, aloof or irritable. The argument that it is impossible to break bad news well has been refuted by Cunningham *et al.* (1984) who found the rate of parental satisfaction with disclosure to be dramatically enhanced by appropriate professional policy and training.

As we will discuss below, parental adaptation is also crucially influenced by their perceptions of themselves and their own competence; they need to believe in themselves and their own ability. If we communicate well as professionals, and in so doing we treat parents with respect, they may feel more respect for themselves, and will consequently be more able to adapt. The awe in which we, as professionals, are held by parents frightens me, since this implies that we are perceived as more important, competent, knowledgeable and skilled than parents. A mother's recent comment of, 'I'm just a parent', when introducing herself to me at the beginning of a counselling course, endorsed this point for me. In reality, the role of parent is every bit as demanding, time-consuming and difficult as that of the professional.

Constructions of the child

Adaptation to the diagnosis will also involve major changes in the ways parents construe the child. The most obvious change is the reconstruction of their view of the child who is now ill or disabled, as opposed to being healthy. Enormous anxiety will be associated with this, as the implications of being unhealthy are at first unknown, and will only unfold slowly.

This means that at first the parents will be unable to make predictions about what will happen to the child. They may not have answers to whether the child will live, or for how long; whether he/she will have pain; whether she/he will develop normally or be disfigured. The possibilities for parental concern are endless. They include concerns about the child's happiness and the social implications of the disease. The child may miss school, be isolated from friends or may be rejected by other people. One father was devastated by his daughter telling him that children in her class would not hold her hand because of her eczema. The uncertainty in all this may be as crippling for parents as the reality when the prognosis is bad.

As time passes, anxieties usually lessen as parents gain information about the illness and discover how the child reacts. The fears are, however, easily resurrected with each renewed crisis as the illness progresses.

Changes in the way parents construe their child will depend upon the reactions of the child as well as the constructions they had about the child prior to the illness. Some constructs may not change and all parents react differently. Many have concern for the happiness of the child above all else, and find pain, disability or limited freedom of choice particularly difficult to face. Those who construe their child as all perfect, have considerable changes to make.

Whatever the specific issue, the major concerns are often with the future, and not so much with the present. Parents can see their child now, but they can only guess at the future. One mother's sole concern was with her daughter's looks, another with whether her son would be able to go to university, and another with whether diabetes would stop her daughter from marrying and having children.

In a general way, the adaptation process is the discovery of the extent to which disease has changed the child. Parents can be seen as testing the extent to which previous constructions of the child are still relevant. It can feel as if the process of bonding/attachment is happening all over again. For example, parents sometimes describe the feeling that they have a different child from the one that was separated from them by coma, surgery or the ventilator. This may include feeling that the child has somehow grown up suddenly, if only in the sense that he/she has had experiences beyond those of the parent.

It is important to note here that children are also having to adapt to the disease and to rebuild their construct systems, in terms of the disease, professionals, themselves, and the others in their lives. Children are changing, each in their own unique ways, and a major issue for parents is to understand these changes and to help, not hinder their children. This means that parents not only have to overcome their own difficulties, but need to have done so to such an extent that they can communicate openly with their children in order to prepare them for what is to happen. The skills of doing this are essentially the same as those used by professionals to communicate with parents. It is therefore appropriate that professionals should explicitly share these skills with parents if necessary.

Parents will be involved in preparing the child for hospitalization, for the pain of injections and venepuncture, chemotherapy, cardiac catheterization, wound debridement or bone-marrow aspirations. Coping with all such events is improved by preparation, and a variety of methods have been used. These include: giving appropriate information and explanation, either verbally, by book or by film; prior modelling of situations; providing strategies for coping with the pain (for example, breathing exercises, positive self-talk, distraction and relaxation); the child being involved in the procedure and being given some control by holding the syringe or using the antiseptic swab. These techniques can be implemented by professional staff but are facilitated by parental involvement. Honest and open communication with the child is vital and information must be given in ways that the child can understand and use.

Parents frequently fail to distinguish between constructions of the child and the illness, as demonstrated in the child characterization sketch presented earlier in the chapter. Another very distressed father described himself as 'unable to see my daughter'; all he saw was the condition of her arthritis: 'I never look at *her*, or ask her how *she* is, when she wakes up or comes home from school. I don't see her; I see her pain and her limp. I'm happy and love her when she's well, and I get angry and snappy when she's not'. Such confusions have clear implications for the behaviour of the parents and consequently for the child. In cases like this, selective denial of the disease or aspects of it, may be the only way that parents can cope, can see the child as a child, and can therefore begin to provide a normal environment for him/her.

A further problem that may arise from the confusion of the child and the disease is that of over-protection, or unnecessarily restricting the range of experiences to which a child is exposed. No doubt some restriction is vital, to reduce the risk of injury in haemophilia, for example, but this has to be balanced against the needs of the child in terms of learning opportunities. There is a tendency not to communicate openly with the child about all aspects of the illness or to involve him or her in decision-making. This is especially important in circumstances where the disease is potentially fatal and the treatment outcome uncertain. A particular difficulty may be the failure to discipline consistently and appropriately a child who is ill. This may arise from a number of constructions, such as perceiving the child to be in constant danger, believing that the child has too many other troubles with which to contend, or feeling that punishment only adds to the gross unfairness of the disease.

Such constructions and the resulting parental behaviours are significant in that they disadvantage both child and parents. The child may fail to acquire a variety of skills, or may not learn to cooperate with others or to share. A restricted and self-centred view of the world may develop which can inhibit the child's ability to relate and be attractive to other people. In the short-term, a major problem that occurs with considerable frequency is the development of various behaviour problems that can disrupt family functioning to an enormous degree, exaggerate the difficulties already being experienced by the family as a result of the illness, tax the parents' ability to love the child, and affect the parents' and child's relationship with siblings. Behaviour problems may also disturb the physical treatment of the child, in that parents may be unable to get the child to wear spectacles, use a hearing aid, take prescribed drugs or undergo painful procedures without excessive resistance.

Overcoming such problems is very much a process of helping parents to understand the ways that the child is making sense of events. They have to work at developing their own understanding of the constructions used by the child.

Self-constructions

The ways in which we construe ourselves are central determinants of all our behaviour. Parents' self-constructions are a vital part of the process of adapting to disease. These constructions are likely to change in the crisis of disease, and they do so in ways which are frequently problematic. Parental distress is frequently associated with these self-constructions, for example, in feeling they caused or could have prevented the disease, or feeling they should be able to take the illness or disability away but cannot. Certainly their behaviour to their children is usually as much determined by the way they perceive themselves and their role, as by their constructions of the child's needs or behaviour. Some parents define themselves and their role exclusively with reference to their children whereas it may be more adaptive to keep them separated to some extent. A mother might construe her child as being naughty, but would not be able to act appropriately because she views discipline as increasing the child's adversity in the context of illness. She may construe discipline as selfishness, if she sees the parental role as one which makes no demands and responds only to the needs of the child.

The diagnosis potentially changes fundamental beliefs parents have about their child, and therefore has major consequences for the ways they construe themselves. They may question their own competence in the past, the present and the future; they may explore their own role in the causation of the disease; they may question whether they can cope with the distress of the situation generally; and they may feel helpless and hopeless about taking the problems away from their child. Some mothers with whom I work have had fundamental doubts about themselves as women, mothers and wives, either before or as a result of the illness, and this has decreased their ability to cope. The fact that many mothers may have to give up work outside the home can have negative consequences, given that their jobs often provide self-esteem and evidence of independence, creativity and/or productivity.

To be effective in any capacity, we require a degree of self-confidence. If I do not feel good about myself, I am likely to have difficulty in adapting to any situation that is remotely demanding. I must have a basic acceptance of myself or feel good about myself in a realistic way, and believe in my ability (what Bandura called self-efficacy) if I am to adapt reasonably, no matter what the circumstances. The need for these basic requirements becomes all the more pressing in circumstances that are threatening and stressful, as in the case of dealing with the initial crisis of chronic disease and the demands this may make, year after year. Lack of self-esteem and self-efficacy are related to depression and anxiety. Poor self-esteem, in itself, will hinder adaptation and therefore increase the difficulties experienced so that a downward spiral is created, with the ability to cope being more and more eroded. Concurrent stresses such as parental ill-health, unemployment, financial problems or other bereavements, may further increase the demands upon parents, and may further decrease their self-esteem.

The very fact of the child's disease makes some parents doubt themselves. They frequently test the hypothesis that there is something they did that caused the problem, be it a pre-term birth, Down's syndrome, cerebral palsy or a heart condition. Their contribution to a genetic condition may be sufficient ammunition with which to punish themselves. They may search for what they failed to do that might have prevented the problem.

Parents have a very strong and natural desire to cure their child completely, and the fact that this is frequently impossible is an important element in undermining self-esteem. A father who construes himself as being in control of events, as protecting his child from harm, as a problem-solver, a remover of hurt and as provider for the child's future, must adapt dramatically in the context of serious disease, or else suffer feelings of inadequacy and helplessness. Parents of children with chronic diseases are not able to produce cures. Instead, they have to learn to suffer *with* the child, and not to suffer *for* the child. The child is having to cope with the disease just as they are, and it will help if they accept the reality of the disease as best they can. This means accepting that the problem cannot magically disappear, that the child must cope, and respecting that he or she will do so. Parents should recognize that the process will be facilitated by close sharing. They frequently talk of the waiting that is a constant part of disease: waiting for the diagnosis or for test results; waiting for the child to regain consciousness or to return from the operating theatre; waiting to see if skills will come back after head injury or major viral infection. This at once illustrates their helplessness and dependence, and the need for personal strength and the strategies to find relaxation and peace.

The process of learning to accept the disease is not easy. If we are not careful, professional competence may inadvertently further reduce parents' own self-competence. The health visitor's instructions about breast-feeding may simply highlight the mother's own inadequacy. The surgeon's skills may be the stimulus for a father to question the role he played in keeping his baby alive ('What did I do to save her?'). The psychologist's knowledge of behaviour problems may similarly demonstrate parental inadequacy.

In conclusion, although the explicit problems presented to professionals are most likely to revolve around the child, the illness and treatment, a central issue remains the self-constructions of parents. These may not be raised spontaneously, but must be addressed, because they reflect upon the parents' ability to cope with the whole situation.

Constructions of partner

Having a child with a serious and chronic illness has many implications for the relationship between parents (where there are two in a family). The way in which parents cope as a couple, will at least partly be influenced by the nature of their relationship prior to the illness. Whatever the situation, the possibility of increased stress upon the relationship is very high, and changes must occur. Couples may be preoccupied with worries and have less time for each other. As a result, fewer of their needs (emotional, practical, sexual, social or intellectual) will be met by their partner. Sabbeth and Leventhal (1984) have shown that there is increased disharmony between parents of children who are chronically ill or disabled, but although this can result in marital breakup, the frequency of divorce is not increased.

The presence of only one parent in a family can be a major source of stress, because of the absence of the support that a partner can give in psychological, economic and practical terms. This does not mean that problems will inevitably arise where there is a single parent, and the level of family adaptation may be superior to a situation where a couple are in conflict.

In working with parents whose children are seriously ill or disabled, relationship problems are a frequent topic. The routine care of the child still tends to fall mainly on the mother, who may feel unsupported by her husband who, in turn, may complain of limited attention from his wife. A particularly difficult issue is when one parent construes the other as in some way to blame for the illness. Another problem concerns disagreement about the treatment. Such difficulties may be exacerbated by the fact that one parent, usually the father, rarely has contact with professionals caring for the child, and so may be deprived of one source of support and/or insight.

Constructions of the siblings

As in other areas, the parents' constructions of their other children (the siblings of the child who is ill) and of their relationship with them are likely to change. A frequent concern, if not a reality, is the extent to which the other children are neglected. The child who is ill will command increased attention, so that parents may not respond adequately to the needs of the siblings. They may be aware of construing the problems of their healthy children as trivial and irritating.

Some families deal with this neglect by a division of labour, with, for example, the father taking particular care of the siblings. Although this may help the children, parents may still experience sadness at the loss of family outings, the loss of a happy-go-lucky atmosphere, or the lack of time resulting from extra demands upon them. In cases where neglect of siblings is not addressed, serious behaviour problems may result.

Constructions of other people

How the parents construe others, such as family, friends and neighbours, will certainly be reviewed and may change after the diagnosis of their child's illness. Pre-existing difficulties may be resurrected or exaggerated. An initial difficulty may relate to informing others of the diagnosis. One mother found it impossible to tell her own parents about a rare inherited metabolic disease, because they were old and had already suffered several tragedies in their lives. The secret was relatively easy to keep as she had emigrated to another country. However, it became a crisis when her parents decided to visit several years after the birth of the child. In another family, the husband's parents were not informed because of the wife's belief that they viewed her as inferior to their son, who should never have married her. When they eventually discovered the truth, they were indeed difficult and unsupportive, at least partly as a result of not being informed! A Muslim family kept the fact that their child had Down's syndrome secret, because they believed that this would be seen as a sign of their sinfulness and that others would think badly of them.

Some families become very isolated as a result of the disease. This may be due to personal psychological difficulties (poor self-esteem, extreme anxiety or depression); pre-occupation with the child; financial problems; or because of the failure to find a child minder who can be entrusted with the child and who can cope with emergencies such as epileptic seizures. Some families deliberately withdraw, because of the disappointment they feel towards others who do not seem to appreciate the difficulties they face, or avoid them because they do not know what to say or how to help. Parents have different reactions to such problems: they may feel anger toward strangers who stare at the child, they may feel embarrassment because of the seemingly odd behaviour of their child, or they may feel frustration at the constant need to explain the problem to whoever is present.

Fortunately many families find their social networks positive and supportive. Research in this area shows that social support is a major factor in good adaptation. Such support is important in a variety of ways: it provides practical assistance, distraction and has a positive effect on the self-esteem of parents. Other parents of children who are chronically ill or disabled may become a new source of support, provided parents want to meet each other and do so on their own terms.

Daily life

Parental constructions of all other aspects of their lives are likely to change, if only in terms of their relative importance. Routines for the management of the home and family may have to be reconsidered and changed when a child is chronically ill, for example, to accommodate regular tests and treatment schedules. There may be considerable disruption with time spent in hospital and days missed from school and work. The housework, shopping and all other household tasks become difficult, and parents may be forced to reconstrue priorities. The cleanliness of the house and the tidiness of the garden may be perceived as of little consequence compared to looking after the needs of the child who is ill. Care of the other children can be a major issue, for example, when a child is transferred from a local hospital to a regional centre for specialized care. Major structural changes may be required to accommodate a wheelchair, lifts or handrails. Families may even have to move.

One or both parents may have to cut down work hours or give up employment, perhaps losing the satisfaction of a challenging career in order to look after the child. Working parents are likely to have reduced attention, motivation and fulfilment. Such changes have obvious financial implications, which are potentially difficult given the increased costs involved in illness (for example, transport and equipment). There are also psychological implications, given the fact that people derive a variety of rewards from their work, including interest, status, self-esteem and companionship.

There may be much less time available for other activities, either for the family as a whole or for individual members – and this has implications for all aspects of life including relationships, aims, values and self-conceptions. Not being able to go to the sports club was a major issue for a mother who, until the time of her child's illness, had been a promising athlete. Ambitions for a bigger house or better car may be lost, with the possible accompaniment of resentment and disappointment. For others the change may eventually be positive with the realization that the search for material possessions is of little significance compared to health and relationships.

Meaning of life

This last point brings us to a final aspect of the construct system which relates to the parents' overall philosophy and purpose for living. All of us have constructions about the meaning of life, the reasons we are here and what will happen when we die. These are important constructions and have a bearing on the way we think of ourselves and our relationships with others.

Such constructions will certainly be examined deeply by parents in the context of chronic disease. The question of why it should have been their son/daughter who became ill will almost inevitably arise. The constructions parents have about the existence of God, the fairness and justice of life, and the reasons for living will be questioned. Some give up their faith in God, whilst others seek the solace that this provides. Others will not change their basic faith, but they do have to reconsider how to make sense of the tragedy that has befallen their child.

'I am not religious but I do believe in some sort of collective consciousness, and ... I found myself spending more time ... begging whatever spirits there were in nature to let my son live.'

(Byard 1991, p.51)

Belief in God and the afterlife is a construct system that can provide meaning in adversity and enormous support and comfort. However, there are some parents for whom such beliefs generate additional problems. Parents have been known, for example, to be misled into expecting miracles by so-called religious advisers. One father spent much of his time praying in order to achieve the perfect image of his child in his mind as a way of obtaining a cure for cerebral palsy. Unfortunately his obsession with this pursuit, resulted in problems for the family centred around the relationship between him and his wife.

Concluding Remarks

If one is to help parents to adapt to chronic disease and disability, it is important to begin with some conception of the situation confronting them. Although most parents are resilient and strong, and cope better than one might ever expect, they and all other members of their family face many difficulties and experience much by way of stress and distress. In this chapter, therefore, I have explored the situation from the viewpoint of the parents, because it is their view that will have a major influence upon all that occurs within the family. The parents are ultimately responsible for what is done for the child, in terms of the illness and his/her total well-being. The wishes, abilities and well-being of the parents in all aspects of their lives cannot be ignored because, if neglected, it may be to the detriment of the child and the treatment of her/his illness.

Although the focus is upon the parents, it is important to note, however, that the processes occurring in the parents are simultaneously happening in all family members, not forgetting for one moment the child who is ill or disabled. The framework for understanding the adaptation of the parents is equally applicable to the child and the other members of the family. It can be used as a basis for helping children directly in terms of professional–child communication, or in helping parents understand, communicate effectively with, and support their children themselves.

With this framework in mind, I will now go on to consider how to provide help. Professionals may not be aware of many of the psychosocial problems experienced by the family. Unless these problems are extreme, they are frequently hidden from view, as parents are inclined to protect professionals from their non-physical difficulties. This is because they do not expect the professional to be able to help, and because of the tendency in all of us not to admit psychosocial difficulties as we think these reflect negatively upon ourselves as people. Nevertheless, most parents do want someone to whom they can talk, and there is much that we can all do to help just by being with them and listening to what they feel without having to take away their hurt. The gap that frequently separates professional and parent can be reduced or completely removed by effective professional communication skills. The effect of reducing the gap is improved support for parents and, in turn, a better quality of life for all members of the family, including the child with the disease.

Summary

❏ The occurrence of chronic disease or disability in a child is a major source of stress and distress to which all members of the family must adapt.

❏ The provision of psychosocial help requires an understanding of the effects of disease, the processes of adaptation, and the family problems experienced.

❏ Research studies indicate high rates of psychological and social disturbance in children with chronic disease, their parents, and siblings.

❏ Marital difficulties are increased and the functioning of the family unit may be disrupted.

❏ Factors predicting adaptation difficulties may include characteristics of the disease (CNS involvement, visibility, disability, possible fatality, pain), child age, family stability and communication patterns, parental physical and emotional health, concurrent stress, and social and emotional support.

❏ To enable understanding of the adaptation processes, it is assumed that all individuals make sense of the events of their world by constructing a model (construct system) which permits anticipation of what is likely to happen and what the appropriate response should be.

❏ The onset of disease is seen as a crisis that invalidates the individual's existing model, or renders its validity uncertain.

❏ The adaptation process can be seen as the exploration of the implications of the disease for the individual, and the consequent rebuilding and modification of the existing construct system.

❏ It is a process that takes considerable time, is undoubtedly painful, and involves all aspects of the person's life.

❏ Particularly important areas of change in the parent's construct system relate to: the disease, the professionals involved, the child, self, spouse/partner, siblings, other relevant people, all aspects of daily routines and philosophy of life.

❏ The problems a particular parent will face are unique, but can be understood and assessed in relation to the important areas of their construct system.

3

Helping: Aims, Relationship and Process

'Don't keep telling me what to do. Help me find out for myself.'
(A mother whose child has sickle cell anaemia)

There are few people working as specialist counsellors in child health, and very few families are referred to external agencies for psychosocial help. Given so few resources and the failure to use external facilities, every member of staff, from the receptionist to the paediatrician, must be aware of the psychosocial effects of disease in all the families they see, and must try to help. Professionals (in the health, education and social services) could help more effectively if there were: 1) appropriate policies giving priority to psychosocial care (see Chapter seven); 2) common and explicit aims for all service personnel; 3) systematic allocation of resources; and 4) basic training in the frameworks and skills described in this book. In this chapter, we will begin with a consideration of the aims appropriate to a broader view of helping, and will provide an outline of the helping process as a guide to the rest of the book. The nature of the relationship between the parents and professional is emphasized as an essential ingredient of the helping process.

Aims of Helping

There are three general aims of helping that I would like to suggest. I have deliberately focused on the parents, because the treatment enterprise is, to a very large extent, dependent upon their commitment and competence.

1. To facilitate the ways in which the parents and all other family members adapt to the child and the disease, psychologically, socially, physically and in their everyday lives, minimizing or preventing disruption as far as is possible.

2. To enable the parents and other family members as best they can to meet the needs of the child who is ill or disabled, without neglecting their own needs.

3. To enable the child who is ill to have the best possible quality of life, by curing the disease if possible, or by at least preventing or minimizing the adverse physical effects. This involves reducing disability and handicap, and facilitating the child's adaptation to the disease – psychologically, socially and in the tasks and pursuits of everyday life.

Specific objectives of helping

These aims translate into a series of specific objectives that will differ from family to family, depending upon their particular characteristics, the problems they have and their wishes and goals which have to be negotiated. Nevertheless, I have generated a list of points to be considered with all families and excluded as necessary. The points focus on the parents but the helper might apply these objectives to other members of the family, including the child who is ill, with the explicit permission of the parents. Specific objectives of helping are:

➤ to support the parents emotionally and socially throughout the adaptation process, encouraging them in all they do;

➤ to enhance their self-esteem; helping them feel good about themselves;

➤ to increase their feelings of self-efficacy, enabling them to feel in control and able to cope;

➤ to help them to explore their situation, so that they will be better able to understand and anticipate events, in terms of the disease and its consequences generally;

➤ to enable them to communicate effectively with and support the child who is ill or disabled, so as to maximize her/his psychological and physical well-being;

➤ to enable them to develop general coping strategies, allowing them to analyse problems, determine options and devise ways of dealing with any situations that may arise;

➤ where there are two parents in the family, to help them feel good about each other and to encourage open communication and mutual support;

➤ to enable parents to find their own support systems as necessary outside the immediate family;

➤ to help them communicate appropriately with professionals in order to work in partnership;

➤ to enable them to make decisions for themselves, in consultation as necessary, and to foster independence.

It is important that all members of a service think carefully about their general aims and objectives and reach a consensus about what they want to achieve. It can be argued that time is not available for such team discussion, but in its absence it is impossible to know the extent to which team members share common goals, how to allocate resources appropriately and what skills and training are required.

None of the aims listed here can be achieved in the absence of a close relationship and good communication between the family and the professional. Ideally, there should be a specific person designated to form a relationship with the family in order to provide consistency and coordination. Since, in resource terms, this means that every member of a team would have to support a group of families, all team members should be knowledgeable about communicating effectively, should have appropriate skills, and should be supported themselves.

Without such a system, the need for basic counselling skills is even more crucial, so as to provide the best help available in every contact with every family, regardless of the length of the interaction and the specific content of the meeting.

The Partnership Model

Effective help is dependent upon the relationship that develops between the parent and helper. The ideal relationship is a partnership, not a dictatorship in which the professional, by virtue of knowledge, is assumed to be superior. Although it is not easy to achieve this ideal, because of our own preconceptions and the expectations of parents, it is important to try. To do this properly requires that we have an explicit understanding of the nature of the relationship for which we strive. It also entails negotiation with parents in order to clarify their expectations and to establish joint aims. We may need, for example, to negotiate a broader concern to do with the adaptation and quality of life of all members of the family, as opposed to a narrow focus upon the child's disease. It is advisable to help parents understand that professionals are not omnipotent or omniscient. We may also need to negotiate the ingredients of a successful relationship, the elements of which are described below.

Working closely. The first implication of partnership is that those involved work together. It is not possible for one person alone to do all the work of investigating, making decisions and carrying out treatment. Successful outcomes require that both the professional and the parent are involved, with a commitment to work hard and to the best of their ability. The more closely they work, the better the outcome is likely to be.

Common aims. A model of partnership requires that the partners have common goals. If they are to work together, there must be, at the very least, implicit agreement about what they are trying to achieve. Preferably, however, there should be explicit agreement which has been specifically negotiated.

Complementary expertise. Although parents and professionals are clearly different, their expertise and other qualities are complementary and of equal importance. One cannot operate without the other, if the outcomes of their work are to be optimized. The paediatrician could act without the parent, but the effects would be compromised if the parents disagreed, were not consulted or were distressed or dissatisfied.

Professionals and parents differ in their role, personality, values, concerns and training. The professional is usually more knowledgeable about disease. Parents will not have such expertise at the beginning, although eventually they can match or occasionally surpass that of the clinician. Nevertheless, they do have knowledge and skills that are crucial to the health care process. They know their child. They are therefore the best judges of both physical and psychological changes in terms of symptom development, side-effects and improvements. They are more likely to know what the child would like or will tolerate, how to communicate with him/her and how to comfort. They are also more knowledgeable about themselves: their own aims and values, their knowledge and skills, and their strengths, weaknesses and difficulties. They are, in fact, the only people who can decide what they want for their child and family.

Mutual respect. To be successful, a partnership requires mutual respect. It is crucial, and will be considered in the next chapter, as a fundamental attribute of helpers. Accepting the notion of complementary expertise is respectful, with both partners accepting the equal importance of the other.

Professionals tend to command respect simply by their title, but it is important that they earn it. Parents, however, should be shown respect, by acceptance of their feelings, their aims, their strengths, their importance to the process of dealing with disease, and their ultimate decision-making role – even when they appear difficult or disagree. It never ceases to amaze me how well parents and their children cope with the most horrific circumstances and are still able to protect us, as professionals, from the pain and distress. Notions of the professional as the wise protector or parent figure are misplaced here.

Negotiation. Although the notion of partnership engenders mutual respect, it is unrealistic to expect either party to be correct all the time, or to assume complete agreement. Disagreements will always occur and must be resolved. However, they are often not acknowledged as conflicts because of the authoritarian relationship that frequently exists. For example, if a clinician prescribes a treatment approach with which the parents disagree, they either keep quiet and simply do not comply, or they question the prescription and run the risk of offending the professional.

Founding the relationship on negotiation, reduces the probability of such events. If everything the professional does were regarded as suggestions, presented for parental consideration and negotiation, and not as given wisdom or command, the relationship would be more open and potentially more effective. The respect that is shown to parents by this more tentative approach, would make parents feel more valued, thereby increasing their regard for the professional, and decreasing the likelihood of disagreement and antagonism, whether overt or covert.

Communication. For a partnership to be successful in terms of all the characteristics listed here, it requires skilled communication. This involves easy, two-way transmission of information in ways understood by all participants. From the viewpoint of the helper, this does not just mean saying something clearly. It implies: 1) providing the circumstances in which the parent/partner can give clear and appropriate information; 2) listening carefully to their message; 3) interpreting it as accurately as possible; and 4) responding appropriately.

Honesty. Implicit in the characteristics of a partnership already mentioned, but worth making explicit, is the need for honesty. There must be an assumption on both sides that all ideas, feelings and information relevant to their joint endeavour will be shared accurately and openly, even when the information is not good.

Flexibility. A final characteristic of the relationship assumed in the partnership model being advocated, is flexibility. Although consistency and stability are ingredients for success, the relationship must be flexible enough to adapt to what is negotiated with parents, and to changes in the parents and their circumstances. This includes, for example, parents' emotional ups and downs, their changing coping strategies and the development of their own alternative sources of support.

Adopting a partnership model does not guarantee the acquisition of the specific skills necessary for helping parents, but it is likely to move us in the right direction. Communication will be enhanced, because parents will have the chance to speak and be heard. The helper will have more information as a result, and therefore be more able to diagnose and treat effectively. Parents will be better informed, more satisfied and compliant, and more able to deal with the disease. They will feel more involved, more in control and more effective, further contributing to their general level of adaptation.

The Expert Model: a Contrast

To be effective, each helper must have a clear picture or model of the kind of relationship for which they strive, yet many of us do not explore these aspects of our work. It is, however, important to do so, because our assumptions affect our interactions with the people we try to help. To illustrate, let me briefly describe what is perhaps the most common model implicit in most of our professional behaviour. It is the expert model, which contrasts sharply with the notion of partnership discussed above.

This model involves the assumption that we, as professionals, should be the experts, and that it is our responsibility to solve the parents' problems. We feel we have to alleviate any and all difficulties and, if we do not, we are failing in our task. Such a view is always with us as a pressure. Even though it is not the model that I accept, I still feel a responsibility to try to solve problems for parents, even when this is impossible. I cannot take away their pain and grief when a child is disabled or dies, but I still feel the desire to try.

The problems with this model are twofold. Firstly, if we aim for the impossible, we will automatically and always fail. This has the consequence of making us feel ineffective or unsuccessful, and we are likely to try to avoid such situations in the future. For example, we might avoid listening to the distresses that parents have simply because we feel we cannot help, even though listening to and being with the parent is, in itself, helpful.

Secondly, the expert model leads to professional behaviour that is detrimental to parents and the helping process, partly because it is unrealistic (for example, relatively little is known about chronic disease) and partly because it is motivated by defensiveness. The professional with an expert model takes over control (asks the questions, makes the decisions, and takes or dictates the actions). Such behaviour has the effect of indicating the superiority of the helper, and thereby casting doubt upon the expertise of the parent. This can undermine parents' self-esteem, which will decrease their ability to adapt. It can make them dependent upon the professional and increase their passivity, thereby decreasing their contribution to the treatment process. As a result, the expert will consult them less thoughtfully and carefully, negotiate less, gather less adequate diagnostic information, and provide less effective and less acceptable advice. Lowered respect for parents increases the likelihood of parents being treated as vulnerable and in need of protection. Professional behaviour will be more inflexible because there rarely will be feedback from parents to encourage the professional to reconsider a decision.

The expert model is, in my view, unhelpful and inappropriate. It does not facilitate a close working relationship. As a consequence, it will not facilitate the realization of many of the aims and objectives that are considered here.

The Process of Helping

The nature of the professional–parent relationship is developed within the context of the whole process of helping, which includes the establishment of the helping relationship and the use to which it is put. We have a choice of many different approaches to helping derived from theories of counselling and psychotherapy. A comprehensive description of alternatives can be found in Patterson (1986), although a much simpler description of the five most influential theories is given by Davis and Fallowfield (1991c).

The approach to be adopted here has been very much influenced by the work of Gerard Egan (1982). The importance of his model is: 1) it is extremely clear in presentation; 2) it is orientated to the practical questions of what the helper should do at each stage to enable people to manage whatever problems they face; and 3) it is integrative in that it provides a framework that can encompass many useful aspects of other theories, including the important work of Carl Rogers (for example, Rogers, 1959) and the work of George Kelly (1991) to whom I have referred already.

I would like to represent the helping process as a sequence of stages or, more accurately, tasks (see flow diagram). It is a model that I have found personally useful in working with families, and have used as a basis for professional training. The model is not fixed in stone, but is intended as a working guide to the complexity of the helping situation. It is kept simple deliberately and must be considered flexibly. For example, all the tasks may not be appropriate to all people. It may be that only the first two stages of relationship building and exploration will be necessary to facilitate parental adaptation. In other instances, where there are multiple problems, one may have to consider all the stages for each of the problems in turn. The stages should also be seen flexibly in that, at times, one may have to backtrack to an earlier task in order to progress.

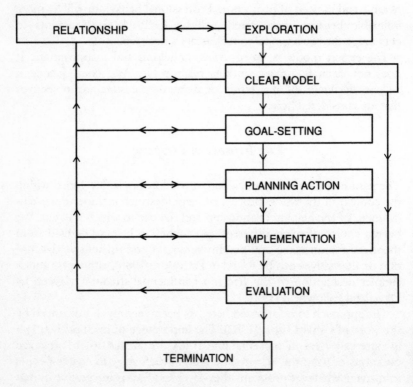

Diagrammatic representation of the stages in the helping process

Each task will be described briefly here, and will be elaborated in the rest of the book in relation to the skills and qualities required of the helper. The first step, and the prerequisite of everything else, is to establish the parent–helper relationship.

Relationship building

The relationship between parent and helper, like any other, takes time to develop. When people meet for the first time, they are unsure of the situation and not particularly comfortable – especially in the circumstances of being vulnerable and requiring help from a professional who is likely to be seen as an authority figure. To communicate meaningfully and effectively requires that this initial reserve or anxiety be overcome. To work together, people must feel comfortable, and therefore the initial task is to get to know each other as quickly as possible. This is, of course, a process in which both parent and professional build up appropriate constructions of each other.

The task of relationship building is often acknowledged in professional training, but is not given the attention it deserves. The specific difficulties all professionals have in working with others are frequently to do with the absence of an appropriate relationship. Reasons for this include:

- the helper's lack of an appropriate model (for example, the expert model may be used automatically);
- the lack of appropriate relationship-forming skills;
- helpers' anxieties about their skills and role in dealing with psychosocial problems;
- severe psychological difficulties (for example, depression) in parents that prevent them relating to others;
- deep-seated parental distrust, derived from unsatisfactory past experiences with professionals.

Parents seeking help are usually vulnerable. They have problems that are, in themselves, distressing; they will be uncertain of the future and what they should do; they will be unsure of themselves, the setting (for example, clinic or ward) and of the helper. The situation of needing help may be novel to them. They may not be used to disclosing intimate aspects of their lives and may feel embarrassed to admit psychological and social difficulties. People frequently, therefore, begin with statements such as, 'You may think this is silly, but . . .' or 'It's hardly worth mentioning, but . . .'.

Before parents can open up and express what is important to them, they need to know that they can trust the helper not to judge them harshly or laugh at them. They have to learn that they will be respected, shown care and helped. Most people have these concerns, but they differ dramatically in how long it takes for them to establish basic trust and engage in the relationship. For some it will be a matter of minutes, for others several hours. One mother interacted for about ten hours with a very skilled counsellor, before she was able to talk about the real problems she was having with her husband. She later explained that she had difficulties trusting men because of being raped in her teens and treated badly by the police and a social worker. As a result, she had low self-esteem and felt that everyone thought she was bad, including professionals.

The process of establishing the relationship is mutual, and the basic tasks are for the helper and parents to get to know and trust each other as quickly as possible. From the viewpoint of the helper, this involves:

1. Introducing him/herself.
2. Describing his/her role.
3. Coming to a basic agreement about working together.
4. Agreeing what they will do and how.
5. Demonstrating characteristics that indicate he/she may be trusted, good to work with and useful.

These tasks can be seen as the initial stage of a process of development that will continue to evolve throughout the contact between the helper and parents. Professionals, in particular, often assume that parents know who they are, what they do and what to expect, and that they will respect, like and find them useful. However, this is frequently not true, and it is important to be as explicit and as clear as possible. The first stage of the relationship involves the negotiation of an initial contract, which will be subsequently renegotiated at various times so as to gain clarity and complete agreement. If the relationship develops appropriately, the parents will feel in an increasingly strong position to be frank, to question the helper and to negotiate. The deeper and quicker the relationship is formed, the more help one can give.

To summarize, the establishment of a good parent–helper relationship is the beginning of the helping process and vital to the success of the whole enterprise; it also has an important therapeutic function.

A major aim of helping is to provide emotional and social support for parents, and close relationships are extremely supportive in their own right, as research has shown. There are many situations in which the helper can do little apart from giving support. This may occur, for example, at major crisis points, such as the breaking of bad news and at the death of a child. The better the relationship, the more support is likely to be available. Enormous benefit is derived from having someone we respect quietly sitting with us when we are in trouble; someone who will not try to take the problem away or make demands on us.

When in difficulty, it is very easy for us to think badly of ourselves; to think we are failing or worthless. Information that contradicts this tendency is required, and this derives largely from the people around us. If people treat us with respect, as valuable and important (by listening to us or freely giving us their time), then we may maintain or even increase our own self-esteem. If the person is someone with whom we have a good relationship, is someone we trust and respect, then we are more likely to value them, to listen to them and to be influenced by the respect and attention that they provide.

Exploration, clarification and change

This stage begins from the point at which the helper and parent meet, and develops in parallel with the formation of a working relationship. It also contributes to the establishment of the relationship, in indicating to the parents something about the helper's competence and likely value.

The initial step is for the helper and parent to explore the parent's general situation and specific difficulties, with the aim of deriving a clear understanding of them. The helper should avoid making assumptions about the parent at this stage, and should attempt to work with the parent's own perspectives. The task is to enable the parents to look at the model, or construct system, that they use to anticipate the events in their world, to help them derive as clear a picture as possible, and to facilitate change as necessary.

In the first place, this will involve getting a basic statement about the issues or problems as seen by the parents in so far as they are prepared to disclose them at this stage. Once a first description has been achieved, then it can be further and further explored. The problems may be simple and circumscribed or diffuse and wide-ranging. In each case, it is important to consider, but only with the parents' permission, all relevant areas of their construct system as illustrated in the last chapter.

By exploring in this way, the helper will begin to understand the problems confronting the family. It will provide information about what the parents see as problems, what sense they make of them and what explanations they have. The helper attempts to develop a clear picture of the situation facing the family, from their perspective. That is to say, with the advantage of emotional objectivity, the helper constructs a picture or model of the parents' model. At the same time she/he must try to: 1) evaluate the adequacy of the parents' views, in terms of the reality of their constructions, the clarity of their understanding and the presence of misconstructions; 2) share these conclusions with the parents, so as to help them adapt and change.

In one case, a mother attributed her son's failure to cooperate in giving blood samples to his personality ('he was born difficult'), whereas her health visitor felt that he was responding to his mother's extreme anxiety. He never was able to relax in the clinic, especially as his mother did not listen to him, but commanded, scolded and cajoled. Gently sharing this idea with the mother, helped her to explore both possibilities and to change.

Alternative explanations generated by the helper should be shared in a respectful and tentative way. The implication should not be that the parent is wrong, but that there may be other explanations or hypotheses worth exploring. The helper's model is not necessarily correct, and has to be evaluated and tested just like any other.

Although this may imply that the process of exploration only occurs via the helper, it should be noted that the opportunity to talk, in itself, gives parents insight. They may clarify their own situation, change their viewpoint, make major decisions, or solve problems themselves, even when the helper has little understanding of their situation. A mother once said to me, 'I did what you said last week, and it worked', despite the fact that I had said nothing at all, only listened to her thoughts and feelings! Parents may change spontaneously by:

Discovering they are valued. Exploration within a trusting relationship with someone who respects and is respected by the parents, may not take away their problems, but frequently has the important consequence of showing them that they are valued. This relates to what I said at the end of the section on relationship building. It has the effect of changing parents' self-image, offsetting the negative ideas they may have about themselves, increasing their self-esteem and building their personal strength.

Discovering they are right. Exploring the parents' situation validates their ideas and therefore enhances their self-esteem and self-efficacy. For example, a mother who previously felt unable to understand her child's aggressive and disobedient behaviour, was helped by the GP to formulate her own explanations that were accepted by him and served as the basis of the subsequent intervention strategies. The acceptance of her ideas led to enormous gains in the mother's confidence, which was subsequently further strengthened by the success of the strategies adopted.

Discovering misconceptions and new perspectives. Not infrequently, parents have spontaneous revelations leading to major changes in perspective. In discussing her son's poorly controlled diabetes, a mother suddenly became aware that she had been making a fundamental error in calculating the number of calories in his diet. In exploring their daughter's unexpected asthma attacks, a couple realized that they only occurred at her grandma's house, where a cat slept on the child's bed when they were not there. A father suddenly realized that in protecting his son, who had mild cerebral palsy, from all unhappiness, he had prevented him from learning to cope with adversity and denied him the satisfaction of being in control.

To conclude, the stage of exploration is important for two reasons. Firstly, the changes exemplified above, derived spontaneously or via the helper, are beneficial in a variety of ways. Parents may feel better about themselves, and more supported, and, therefore, more able to face their difficulties. They may also have a better understanding of their various problems (fewer misconceptions, more information, or revised perspectives) and so be in a better position to cope without further intervention. Secondly, the clarification obtained at this stage, or the new models derived, provide the basis for the next stages of the helping process, namely, the formulation of goals and the plans to achieve them. However, exploration is an ongoing process, continuing as the parent–helper relationship develops, as parents are more prepared to share their innermost thoughts, and as their understanding of the problems evolves.

Goal-setting

Like the first two stages, goal-setting is an ongoing part of helping. It begins at the first contact, when there has to be at least tacit agreement that the helper and parent will meet and try to work together. However, it is only once there has been some exploration of the problems that clear aims can be set and realistic goals devised.

The process of deciding goals should involve honest negotiation and should recognize the parents as the final decision-makers. This entails a pooling of resources and cooperation between helper and parent so that, once again, the parents' self-esteem and self-efficacy are endorsed and they are seen to be respected by the helper.

It is relatively easy to help parents decide their general aims but more difficult to formulate goals. The general aim may be, for example, to improve the parents' relationship with the child. The goals, however, have to be specific and observable outcomes that are adequate, realistic and attainable within a reasonable period of time. For example, the general aim above may include goals such as: the child will greet mother with a smile; they will laugh together; the child will tell mother her worries; or she will be more obedient.

The goals that are set depend on the exploration conducted by the helper and parents, the explanations they derive, and the priorities they have. The clearer the model of the problems they confront, the easier it is to set specific goals. For example, a mother wanted to stop her child's disobedience and, in discussion, came to the relatively simple explanation that it arose because of her own inconsistency in handling him. She never punished his disobedient behaviour but would warn or threaten him or try to ignore his failure to comply with her requests. At other times, she would use persuasion or even cuddle him. She realized this was a result of her feeling desperately sorry for him because he had a serious progressive disease. Further discussion led her to the conclusion that she was not helping/loving her son by being lenient. Clarification of her own role and responsibility, as well as a new understanding of the child's disobedience, enabled her to set her first goal: to become more consistent in disciplining her son.

Another mother decided to spend more time with her husband each evening, when she saw that her preoccupation with the care of her daughter had led to the deterioration of her relationship with her husband and her consequent unhappiness. The goals for the father were to be able to be less nervous of the paediatrician, to be able to ask all the questions he wanted, and to complain of the lack of information if necessary.

In situations where problems are multiple or complex, the question is not only one of deciding goals, but also of determining priorities and the order in which goals will be tackled. One mother, for example, decided that she needed more information about her child's disease as a way of increasing her own competence, before tackling the child's reluctance to go to school or the father's failure to contribute to the child's care. Another family decided that the most pressing goal was to solve their financial difficulties, before finding a more suitable house for their child with severe learning difficulties.

Where the stage of exploration, in itself, is successful in removing presenting problems, the goal to be negotiated may simply be whether to continue the helper–parent relationship. Where exploration has resulted in no useful explanation of the problem, the goal may be to try to find a helpful framework. For example, a mother could only explain her child's extreme aggressive behaviour in terms of severe brain injury as the result of a traffic accident. Since this explanation facilitated no intervention, the health visitor helped the mother to develop a behavioural model that eventually enabled her to reduce aggression by using a system of rewards.

Where exploration results in not one, but several, alternative explanations, the first goal might be to test the value of the different models. For example, a couple disagreed about the reason for their daughter stealing money at school. The mother believed it was because they had neglected her while their youngest son was in hospital, and the father felt it was simply the result of naughtiness. Each explanation implied completely different goals, and so they decided to test each model separately. They began with the mother's, since the father's model implied (at least for him) the use of punishment which might have been completely inappropriate if the mother was right. Following this the agreed goal became that of exploring the relationship between the mother and father!

Planning action

Once goals have been agreed, the next step is to formulate a plan of action. The task is to explore all the possibilities, and come to a decision about the best way of achieving the established goals. An important part of this process, is evaluation of the various costs and benefits of any particular options in order to make the best decision available. It also involves anticipating any problems that are likely to arise and devising ways to cope with them. This may vary from finding ways to cope with the wait for a kidney, to dealing with the side-effects of a particular drug, to calculating the likely cooperation to be expected from other professionals, or to isolating the skills parents will need in order to carry out treatments.

Clearly, thorough preparation will maximize the success of the endeavour. Parents should be helped wherever possible not only to come to decisions themselves, but to generate the various options. Allowing parents to develop strategies themselves, even though it might be easier for the professional to do so, can transform their self-beliefs dramatically and beneficially.

A frequent issue here is to decide who to involve, as well as what to do. Other professionals (such as dieticians or physiotherapists) may be able to help in attaining goals that have been set. Parents should decide, together with the helper, whether they wish to be referred, whether the helper should supply the parents with the information they need or whether a joint visit would be most beneficial. However, it may be that which option is chosen is less important than the way in which it is decided. Preferably this should be by open negotiation with the parent having the final say. This applies also to decisions about implementation of treatment procedures or teaching programmes (for example, for children with learning difficulties), which parents may or may not wish to conduct themselves. It is wise not to make assumptions about what parents want to do. However, whatever their decision, the importance of continuing support is crucial.

Implementing plans

Once clear plans have been formulated, the situation is relatively straightforward. The helper has to do whatever she/he has agreed, but should also monitor what happens. If the parents are to carry out certain procedures themselves, they may need support while they do so. This will be as true for simple drug regimes as for more complex procedures, where there are several drugs, physiotherapy or developmental/behavioural programmes.

Such support may involve meeting parents periodically or keeping in touch by telephone. It must certainly involve praise for success, or encouragement when they are discouraged. Whatever happens, they are likely to have worries and questions at all stages, and will value the chance to explore these. This may be particularly the case when they have been referred to another professional whose communications are unclear, or when there is further bad news.

Evaluation

The final task is evaluation. This may occur constantly in the interaction between the professional and parent. However, it is crucial once some kind of action plan has been instituted, in order to determine the outcomes of the actions taken, and to decide on future steps. Evaluation involves obtaining feedback on the effectiveness of the solutions attempted, but it can also help the parents to get a clearer understanding of their problems, particularly when the outcomes are less than successful.

Given complete success in, for example, reducing a behaviour problem, parents are to be congratulated, with emphasis upon their role in the matter and their effectiveness. Furthermore, it is important to explore this as it may make future problem-solving that much easier for the parents. It may also be the point at which the parents and helper explore their relationship, and decide whether they need to continue meeting or whether to meet less frequently. On the other hand, it may be the point at which they move on to the next goal. For example, once a child with diabetes accepts injections without a struggle, the next step may be to help her do it herself. Having helped the child to adhere to the dietary requirements of a disease, a parent may then want to look at their relationship with the child so as to help them all cope better.

If the actions taken were not successful or only partially so, then the task becomes one of exploring the reasons for the failure. It may be that actions were not carried out properly; that the plan was not adequate; that the goals were inappropriate; that the situation was not understood properly in the first place; or that the relationship between the helper and parent may be problematic.

The evaluation of both the outcome and the process of helping should throw light on what went wrong. It may be discovered, for example, that a father's plan to spend more time with his child failed simply because he had to work more and therefore did not achieve what had been anticipated. Alternatively, the child may have not enjoyed their interactions because the father was tired at the time chosen. In the first case, the remedy would be to wait until the father was available; in the second case, the plan would need to be changed in order to make the interaction more enjoyable. In fact, this influenced the father in that he realized that he could not help his son simply by being with him, but had to learn the skills of interaction with a child of this age. Far from being unsuccessful, the failure here allowed the father to develop and change his construct system about his child so that a close relationship could be formed. This serves to illustrate that the helping process is not a simple path through the stages described, but a more fluid process as illustrated by the flow diagram (see page 42).

Concluding Remarks

In this chapter, I have attempted to give an overview of the aims of helping; the kind of relationship which would facilitate the realization of these aims; and an outline of the helping process in terms of the tasks to be undertaken within the relationship. This model, however, is insufficient on its own – helpers need particular skills and qualities in order to put it into operation. The remainder of the book describes these characteristics in a way that may be helpful to the reader's clinical practice.

Summary

❏ The aims and objectives of helping relate to the facilitation of the well-being of all members of the family – this being a vital ingredient in the treatment of the physical disease of the child.

❏ Of particular importance, are the objectives of enhancing parental self-esteem and self-efficacy, understanding and general coping and problem-solving strategies. The skills of communicating effectively – most particularly with the child, other family members, and professionals – are also emphasized.

❏ The process of helping families hinges upon the quality of the relationship established between the parents and the helper. It is argued that an ideal relationship would be based on the principles of a partnership model (as opposed to an expert model).

❏ A partnership involves working closely, common aims, complementary expertise, respect, negotiation, communication, honesty and flexibility.

❏ As a flexible guide, the process of helping is characterized as a series of stages or tasks.

❏ The stages are: establishing the working partnership, exploration of the situation to formulate clear models, goal-setting on the basis of these models, planning action, implementation and evaluation.

4

Initiation and Exploration

In this chapter I will provide a practical guide to the characteristics that helpers require in order to initiate and establish an effective partnership with parents; and to begin exploring the issues and problems of relevance to them. I will start, however, by considering some general counsellor qualities that are essential to the whole process of helping, before looking in detail at more specific skills. The chapter will conclude with a consideration of the first meeting between the helper and parents, and a short case example by way of illustration.

Fundamental Attitudes

There are a number of qualities that are fundamental to the process of effective counselling. These characteristics were highlighted in the influential pioneering work of Carl Rogers, an excellent summary of which can be found in Rogers (1959). Like Rogers, I refer to these qualities as attitudes to indicate a general and pervasive stance that is taken by skilled helpers towards the people with whom they work. How these characteristics influence the process is complex and will no doubt differ in each case, but Rogers proposed an 'If ... then ...' model. He argued that IF the helper showed these qualities, and the person seeking help was aware of them, THEN that person would change in a beneficial way.

My belief is that these qualities are central to supportive work with parents and, in themselves, provide practical guidance for how we should act in the helping context, regardless of the specific techniques that we might use. I will describe each of these attitudes in turn, using Rogers as a starting point. Although discussed separately here, they are, in practice, all highly interrelated.

Respect

Respect is perhaps the foremost attitude, and relates closely to what Rogers called *unconditional positive regard*, or *warmth*. It is a complex

notion that refers to the helper being non-judgemental; thinking positively about parents without imposing conditions, and regardless of
their problems, status, nationality, values or other personal characteristics. For me, personally, it is even stronger than this, and involves
according them honour or esteem. I feel privileged to be trusted by
parents and allowed to share their lives for a brief time. Respect
means valuing the people with whom I work, treating them as very
important.

The implications of this attitude for the behaviour of helpers are
numerous. It means treating parents with courtesy, and making them
the complete focus of our attention for the time that we are with
them. Respect implies allowing them to speak freely, listening to what
they say and valuing it, even if we disagree. It involves willingly using
all the knowledge and skills that we have to do whatever we can to
help, but it does not mean taking over from them or denying their role
in the process of change.

The last point is crucial. Respecting parents assumes not thinking
less of them for having problems; not thinking that they become any
less capable as people as a result of the problem; and not taking away
from them the responsibility for, and their role in, adapting to and/or
solving the difficulties they face. Parents generally cope, no matter
what the problem. They are stronger and more capable than we think.
For example, although one mother lives in extreme poverty, without a
husband, with two children who are blind and a third dying of cancer,
she not only manages well, she also gives to others, even those who
are more fortunate than herself. According respect to this woman and
all others in similar situations is a precious and powerful gift. Such
examples make a mockery of withholding bad news from parents
because they might be hurt. This, in fact, would be a sign of disrespect.

It is not appropriate as a helper to try to deny parents' problems or
to minimize them in any way, because we may not know what to do.
The role of the helper is to acknowledge and respect the problems,
accept them as real and share them, no matter how disastrous the
situation. It is useless to pretend that everything will be all right, when
it will not. There are times when there is little one can do as a professional, but much as a person, as in bereavement or terminal illness.
The tendency to avoid parents in these situations, or to try to make
everything all right is disrespectful, when all we need to do is to accept
parents and their problems and be with them.

The importance given to respect here does not simply derive from
humanitarian values, but from the belief that it has a number of important functions in facilitating the process of helping, if it is perceived by

the parents. Firstly, it helps parents overcome the humiliation often experienced by those who require help. Secondly, it facilitates the development of an effective working relationship between the helper and the parents. Finally, it is therapeutic in itself. If the helper sincerely demonstrates that the parents are important, valuable, and capable, they are more likely to come to believe this of themselves. This, in turn, will enhance their motivation as well as their ability to cope effectively.

According respect as suggested here is not necessarily easy, and may be extremely difficult. However, the assumption that parents are somehow bad, incapable, or helpless, not only makes it impossible to engage in a meaningful partnership, it makes the situation worse. It may put them down, reinforce their deviant or lowered status, reduce their self-esteem, and therefore decrease their ability to help themselves.

Humility

A second attitude, closely related to respect and an important aspect of helping, is humility. This was not discussed specifically by Rogers, but I see it as crucial to my work in this area, and want to highlight it. It is not a weakness, involving self-denigration, low self-esteem or false modesty; it is a strength, in that it requires being open and realistic about oneself, accepting both one's positive characteristics as well as the weaknesses. It also involves acknowledging the differences between ourselves and others, without assuming inferiority either way.

People with genuine humility are effective helpers, because they are realistic about what they have to offer, aware of their limitations and accepting of the contributions of others, whether parents, children or other professionals in the paediatric team. It enables respect and, in so doing, facilitates the benefits mentioned above. It prevents the helper's own self-importance getting in the way of the helping process, since it is not to the family's advantage to think how wonderful the professional is, if this detracts from the importance of their own contribution. It is also important in the prevention of false expectations. The belief that professionals are all-knowing and all-competent is more to do with wish fulfilment on the part of parents than reality. In truth, knowledge of disease is poor, and cure is rare in chronic illness. If parents have unrealistic expectations, then they are likely to be disappointed sooner or later, and the relationship that is so vital to the process of helping is likely to be severely damaged.

Finally, humility prevents professional defensiveness, which is so damaging to the helping process. Helpers with unrealistic expectations of themselves are likely to have difficulties in communicating openly with parents, are likely to fail to achieve what they expect, and are likely to be easily threatened. This means that they will be unable to adopt a partnership model to relate to parents, and will hide behind the expert model criticized in the last chapter. They are also likely to withdraw as quickly as possible from difficult situations, and therefore not provide the human support of being with parents in real need, when there is nothing concrete to do.

Genuineness

The third fundamental attitude is genuineness, which has been used as an equivalent to Rogers' characteristic of *congruence*. The implication is that the helper should be open to all experiences, so as to perceive them accurately and meaningfully, not distorting them with defenses, personal prejudices and problems. Its importance as a basic characteristic of helping derives from the fact that one of the major aims of helping is to enable the full and careful exploration of the problems and issues facing the parents, so that they may develop a clear model that might optimize their adaptation.

For me, therefore, genuineness implies a group of qualities, which all relate to being *open to experience*, attempting to make sense of events clearly and accurately, and being prepared to change. The helper must try to perceive the meaning intended by the parents and should not impose meaning, by making assumptions that are more related to his or her own constructions, prejudices and biases, than those of the parents. Being genuine involves seeing all their problems clearly, not denying or minimizing them, no matter how remote from one's own experience they appear to be. Since being open to oneself is a prerequisite for this, the characteristic of humility is intimately related to genuineness.

Genuineness also implies honesty and sincerity. This means being genuinely interested in the family and their problems, and being completely trustworthy. This includes telling the truth and not misleading parents. It involves doing everything that one says, when one says, and giving good explanations. It also means admitting ignorance or mistakes. It means being with the parents for their purposes, without the helper's own motives intruding (for example, using the endeavour to bolster the helper's own self-esteem). For the relationship to be effective, the parents must trust the helper completely. They must come to know that the sole reason for the helper's involvement is for the benefit and service of the family. Although this may sometimes include addressing issues that are distressing or hurtful to the family, this should only occur if it is of clear value to them, and then carried out in the most positive and sensitive way.

The issue of confidentiality should be mentioned here, since it is crucial to the development of trust. The helper has to make it clear that *everything* that happens in their interactions and *everything* that is said is completely confidential. It is something to be stated at the beginning and endorsed thereafter. Any communication of any sort with a third party must only occur after explicit negotiation with the parent. Apart from demonstrating genuineness, this has the added benefit of putting the parents firmly in control of the helping process.

Two final aspects of genuineness worth mentioning are spontaneity and consistency. Spontaneity is important, and refers to the helper being able to respond to the parents openly, naturally and freely at all times. Any skills acquired as a means of helping should be fluid, and not laboured, mechanical or artificially deliberate. Consistency refers to the helper not presenting extremely different pictures of him/herself on different occasions. Although we all have changes in mood, dramatic changes are minimized if we are open and unpretentious. Factors that might create inconsistency (for example, helper illness, distress or fatigue), if not otherwise avoidable, should be shared with the parents so that they are not misunderstood. One mother, for example, became distressed because she thought she had upset her health visitor, whereas in reality this usually gifted helper was pre-occupied with troubles of her own.

Empathy

Empathy is Rogers' third major counsellor characteristic. It refers to a general *attempt* by the helper to understand the world from the view-point of the parents. At all stages of the helping process, the helper must try to see the situation through their eyes, acknowledging that it is their constructions that are the basic concern of the relationship, and that it is changes in the parents that are the outcomes to be expected, whatever the views of the helper. The skilled helper must think and feel him/herself into the inner life of the parents, and work with the model that this generates.

I stress the word 'attempt' here because, in reality, it is not possible to understand absolutely the inner world of others (their construct system) no matter how well we know them. Nevertheless, by discussion we can derive an approximation of the models they use. This attitude indicates to parents respect, humility and genuineness and therefore enhances the parent–helper relationship. It is the vehicle by which the problems facing the family are examined in that it guides the exploration in terms of what questions are asked and what directions are pursued. Empathy is thus a significant factor in enabling parents to clarify and change their models.

Discovering the parent's model does not prevent the helper from attempting to evaluate its adequacy once it is available to him/her. It does, however, imply respecting this model and using it as the basis for the interactions, which must involve the helper comparing the parent's model with his/her own. It does not necessarily imply that the helper should agree with the parent, nor does it mean that either the parent or the helper is right or wrong. They might both be right or wrong, but more important, their views are different and these differences are avenues for exploration, clarification, and change. The different models need to be seen clearly before they can be compared and tested.

To illustrate this, one mother construed her son, who had neuromuscular difficulties, as being generally naughty and difficult as a direct result of the disease. In exploring this, the helper found that his misbehaviour was particularly difficult in situations where they had to deal with professionals at the hospital or had to carry out treatment tasks. As a result of this and other observations, the helper formulated an alternative hypothesis, namely that the child resented his mother's sole focus upon his disabilities, showing little overt affection, in her desperate attempt to stop the progression of the illness. She gently shared this new model with the mother, who was initially disconcerted, but experimented with the hypothesis. In so doing, she produced marked improvements in both her son's behaviour and their relationship. She accomplished this by attending to him as a person, listening carefully whenever he wanted to talk and by trying to understand his feelings and to respect what he said. She relaxed, smiled more and showed more affection.

Quiet enthusiasm

Anyone who does a good job has enthusiasm for what they do, whether teacher, mechanic or butcher, and the same is true for the good helper. Enthusiasm is attractive and infectious. It is easily transmitted to parents and their children, and enhances the helper–parent relationship. I suspect that it is professional coldness that often inhibits the development of closer relationships.

I have deliberately said quiet here, because it is inappropriate to be loud and flamboyant when dealing with the serious issues of illness or death, and associated psychological and social problems. Although these problems are sad, it does not mean that the helper must feel sad. In fact, it is appropriate to take pride in what one does and to enjoy doing it well, to the benefit of the recipients. It is possible, for example, to feel good about giving bad news, in the sense that one can be aware of doing an unpleasant job with the care and skill it deserves for the benefit of the person receiving the news. Although the helper's own needs must not overshadow those of the parents, professionals must derive reward from their work, or they will not want to continue and will eventually stop, or suffer 'burn out' as the modern jargon puts it. The person who is unsure of his/her role, preoccupied with personal worries, defensive, pressurized or not absorbed by what is happening here and now in the helping situation, is diluting their effectiveness as a support.

Basic Skills

The specific skills needed for helping are predictable from a knowledge of the fundamental attitudes of respect, humility, genuineness, empathy and enthusiasm. The skills to be described here are pertinent to the first and most important stages of helping: the formation of the parent–helper relationship and initial exploration of the problems presented. However, they are also central to the helper's behaviour at all other stages.

Attending

Perhaps the most basic skill is the ability to attend completely to the parents, to indicate this to them and to exclude all other distractions, including personal worries. Your whole attention should be focused upon the family so that you will be most receptive to what the parents say or imply. Close attending will indicate to parents that you are listening carefully and it will, therefore, facilitate your relationship with them. It provides significant encouragement for parents to begin talking and to continue to do so, in order to explore the issues confronting them.

All aspects of our behaviour, especially the non-verbal, indicate to parents that we are attending. Although it is the whole picture that is seen, it is worth looking briefly at specific cues, which should be carefully regulated by the helper.

Gaze. The most important cue is the direction of our gaze. To be seen to be attending, we must look at the other person somewhere in the region of their face. We do not have to stare without movement, but we do have to indicate a clear pattern of looking. In fact, there is a distinct pattern of looking when people interact, and this has the function of not only providing information, but also of smoothing the interaction. The person listening, looks at the person who is talking most of the time, whereas the speaker shows a variable pattern: looking to get the other's attention, then alternating looking with looking away in a manner depending upon the content of the conversation. If it is simple, the speaker looks more; if complex, he/she looks away more, glancing briefly now and then to check the attention and reaction of the other.

Facial expression. The ever moving pattern of the face tells us an enormous amount about a person, including the direction of their attention. The different ways in which people smile or frown, lift the eyebrows or wrinkle the eyes or nose, provide information about their thoughts, feelings, interests and reactions. We can detect momentary uncertainty, a question, surprise, happiness/sadness, anxiety, interest or anger. People who are interacting monitor each other's face continually for such information.

Body orientation and posture. The general orientation of our body and posture also gives varied information about us. To indicate attention, we must orientate our body in the general direction of the other person, usually at an angle of about 45 to 90 degrees, as opposed to directly face-to-face. The picture we present is further complemented by our posture, which should be comfortable but upright. We should lean slightly towards the other with both feet on the floor. Although one may be able to attend when slouching back or otherwise contorting one's body, it does not provide a receptive picture for the other person.

Relative height is also important. Although it does not indicate attention directly, it can detract from the interaction if people are not at about the same level. For example, it can have status connotations, with the higher person being superior. This may explain the fact that I personally have never been able to do anything about a stoop I have had all my life. I am rather tall, and think that I try not to tower above everyone.

Movement. Movement of all kinds indicates attention or otherwise. Mannerisms, rattling coins, fiddling with a paperclip, swinging one's legs, rocking or drumming one's fingers may indicate inattention, boredom or impatience. They are also distracting to the person talking and contribute little positive to the interaction. On the other hand, attentiveness is not indicated by absolute stillness. It is natural to move slightly all the time and, if we are attending carefully, these slight movements of the head and body tend to be in rhythm with the movements, tempo and conversation of the other person. This is called *interactional synchrony*, and may be a highly significant, albeit unconscious, indicator of attention and interest.

Furthermore, the speed of our reactions in response to another person also provides important information. This includes nodding or shaking our head or even replying verbally. If attending, we usually respond within half a second at the longest. Delays may indicate the listener is thinking carefully, but frequent and excessive delays can be tedious and laborious for the other person, and they can certainly indicate inattention. Used sparingly and carefully, however, pausing can be used very successfully to indicate attention and to keep the person talking.

Paralinguistic cues. A final source of information about a person, comes not only from what they say, but also from how it is said. The speed, responsiveness, fluency and loudness of speech can all indicate that the person is paying attention. The notion of interactional synchrony also applies here, in that the extent to which speech behaviour matches the behaviour of the other is a clear indication of attention. Extreme sorrow, for example, elicits slow and quiet responses if we are attending. Incongruity or interruption can be interpreted as inattention or worse (for example, insensitivity).

Active listening

Related to the skill of attending, is active listening. It is only through listening that the helper can begin to communicate effectively; learn anything of the parent's problems; develop an accurate understanding and so facilitate the rest of the helping process.

I have used the word 'active' to suggest that there is nothing passive about effective listening. It is not simply the attempt to receive verbal information, but an energetic search for the underlying meaning. The constant question for the helper is what do the parents really mean; what sense are they really making of the events in their lives. The effective listener is actively processing all the information available all the time, with the intention of deriving a clear model of the parent's construct system as quickly as possible in all its aspects. This includes hearing the parent's words, how they are said, noting other non-verbal behaviour and noticing what is not shown or said. The helper tries to register the parent's thoughts, feelings and behaviour, whilst at the same time being aware of his/her own reactions to what is occurring. The parent may make us anxious or angry, sad or irritable, and it is important to be aware of these feelings, because they may be relevant.

A mother, for example, complained that hospital staff were being rather curt and avoiding her. While she talked I was aware of feeling a little irritated by her own abrupt manner, and felt threatened by her use of technical terms and her obvious knowledge of the very latest research. Guessing that this was what other staff were feeling, I very carefully shared these thoughts with her, which led her to change her manner allowing her to communicate more effectively with the people on the ward.

As this suggests, the process of listening is more complex than attempting to build up an unbiased picture of the model presented by the parent. It also involves comparison of this with the helper's own models, derived from the whole of his/her experience. To do this, the two (or more) models should be kept clear and separate, with both being treated as theories or hypotheses to be evaluated against each other in order to aid the development of the most useful and clear understanding. This process will be taken up in the next chapter, but another example may help. A woman had come to construe her son as ungrateful for all she had done for him as a result of spina bifida. She focused especially on what she construed as his rejection of her when other parents and children were present. My own tentative construction or hypothesis, based on careful listening, was that the child was trying to assert his independence. Although I could have shared the comparison of the two hypotheses with her, she came to this conclusion on her own as a result of our explorations.

To listen in this way requires that the helper concentrate hard and that distraction be minimized. Obvious sources of distraction are environmental, and depend on the place of the meeting (see page 69). However, it is also important to control distractions that are related to the helper's internal environment. To listen in the way described here, requires that the helper try to clear her/his mind of all irrelevant matters for the duration of the interview. This might vary from an awareness of physical discomfort due to a poor sitting position or a full bladder, to feeling unwell or tired. Worries about our personal lives, pressures upon us, concerns about one's own competence, and thoughts about the previous or next patient, are all to be avoided if one is to give the concentration that is required.

Prompting

Before the helper can listen, the parents must have been given the opportunity to talk. A vital skill of the helper, therefore, is that of prompting, by which I mean enabling the parents to begin talking, encouraging them to continue, and providing some direction. With many parents this is not a problem; they may be naturally talkative and friendly, or their difficulties may be so pressing that they are happy to unburden themselves. With others there may be difficulty initiating a conversation, or of getting them to stop.

In general, simply attending and listening carefully in ways that convey the fundamental qualities described earlier provide the circumstances in which parents are very happy to talk at length. Nevertheless, they will keep checking for reactions, which are clearly indicated by the helper's general manner, but which would include responsive comments like 'Yes', 'mh-mh', or 'I see', and non-verbal behaviour such as nodding the head.

Commonly, the process is initiated with a question such as, 'Why have you come to see me?' or 'How have you been getting on?'. A series of such questions can enable parents to explore their problems comprehensively without further effort. These open-ended questions are very effective in initiating or prompting interactions because they do not limit the answers the parent may provide. The question, 'How has your son been?' invites parents to say whatever they like in response, whereas 'Has your son been well?' is a closed question in that it tends to limit the reply to 'Yes' or 'No'. Given that the aim is to discover the constructions of the parents, then the more open ended the questions, the less likely is the helper to determine the content and direction of the discussions. Closed questioning has a place in acquiring specific information or clarifying points, but extensive use of questioning of this kind is much more authoritarian, and contrary to the notions of partnership.

Other methods of prompting conversation include the use of statements or pauses. For example, a statement like, 'You look much better this week', is as likely as a question to initiate a response, which again may be entirely determined by the parents in both content and length. Particularly effective are statements that are also empathic. Pausing and not saying anything allows parents to continue talking if they wish and can, therefore, be a very effective and non-directive form of prompting. However, if overused or used badly, pauses can be awkward and manipulative, particularly where the situation is novel to the parents and some guidance is required.

A difficult situation arises when the helper has trouble stopping the parent talking, or when the person rambles aimlessly. One can deal with this by becoming a little more directive in questioning, but in extreme cases it might be appropriate to focus upon this, in itself, as one of the parent's problems. It may be that the parent is aware of this difficulty in lots of different situations but has never been able to do anything about it. On the other hand, he/she may never previously have had anyone sympathetic enough or courageous enough to raise it as a problem. To do so requires enormous care, tact and skill.

Perhaps the more common situation is where the person is extremely hesitant or reluctant to talk, and this may arise for a number of different reasons. It may be due to anxieties or uncertainty about the helper situation or because of the novelty of talking about intimate issues. If so, it is important to be patient and reassuring, to allow the parent to control the pace and content of the proceedings, to acknowledge that it is not always easy to talk about difficult problems, and perhaps to address the notion of confidentiality. Undue pressure should not be applied, as this may simply make the situation worse; backing off may indicate that the helper can be trusted sufficiently to begin talking.

Extreme distress is a frequent cause of hesitation, and may be handled by the helper recognizing the depth of feeling and allowing parents to share it if they can. Some reference to what they may be feeling can prompt them to talk, or at least help them to show their feelings directly. An empathic remark such as, 'You seem to be very sad', may enable the person to cry and allow the helper to comfort. Just being quiet, sitting with them and perhaps touching them gently, will often be enough to let them express their feelings verbally or otherwise.

Perhaps the most difficult situation is where the person concerned is extremely depressed or confused and unable to find words or the motivation to talk. There are no simple answers to this, except patience and respect. One can try to prompt in all the ways discussed above, including questioning, but this may only produce monosyllabic answers and can easily degenerate into an inquisition. It may also have the unfortunate consequence of indicating that their reticence is unacceptable, perhaps further endorsing their own negative self-image. My own inclination, however, is to sit quietly with the person and to respond as invited. Sitting with parents like this for half an hour or more, without talking, when parents are in crisis can in retrospect be viewed by them as an extremely powerful experience, like a valued gift. Such experiences have endorsed for me an important principle of helping: that you do not always have to be doing something actively.

Demonstrating empathy

I said earlier that empathy is a fundamental attribute of counselling, because it underpins the process of exploring the constructs that parents use for anticipating events and hence deriving a picture of the world from their viewpoint. However, to be effective in helping, it has to be demonstrated to the parents.

This may be done in a pervasive way by the whole presence of the helper, in attending, listening and enabling parents to talk. More specific and direct, however, is to say something that indicates understanding. Although one might respond by saying, 'I understand', a more effective way is to show one's understanding by describing the parents' thoughts or feelings. This can be done, for example, by paraphrasing the parent's words, and hence reflecting back what they are saying. For example, a physiotherapist said, 'So you were feeling very angry that she was being hurt in this way', when a mother talked about how her daughter with epilepsy had been cruelly teased by children in her class. Another way is to comment on the parent's non-verbal behaviour; for example, 'You looked very anxious (tearful, puzzled . . .) when I said that'.

The skill is to make a short, concise statement that accurately and completely captures what the person is saying, thinking and/or feeling. It does not have to be rushed, but should reflect the parent's tone, manner, tempo and language. Such statements are very powerful and, if not over-used, serve a number of purposes. They are the clearest indicator that the helper is listening carefully. They, therefore, indicate respect, genuineness and, of course, empathy. They also show that the helper is someone who can be trusted to understand and be helpful, and they therefore enhance the parent–helper relationship. This in turn improves the communication between them, so that the helping process is facilitated as a whole. Such statements are also very effective prompts if the conversation flags.

Empathy depends upon very careful listening but, even so, it is not necessarily easy to be completely accurate, and one can be wrong. An analogy is with the game of darts. As long as the dart hits the board it will gain some points, but the most effective is the one that hits the bull. The more accurate the statement, the more effective it is in indicating that you are listening, that you understand and that you care. Hitting the bull's eye can have dramatic effects on parents in helping them accept and clarify their situation.

However, even when inaccurate, empathic remarks are useful in providing the means by which the helper can test her/his understanding of the other person. People are complex, their words and behaviour may be unclear/confused, their non-verbal behaviour may be at odds with what is being said, or the helper may simply not understand. In all such cases, a tentative attempt at empathy allows the parent to give feedback, either validating or contradictory. One mother replied to an attempt at empathy by saying: 'I was sad when her (daughter's) diabetes was diagnosed ... but what really depressed me was my husband's complete indifference'. Always making empathic statements tentative and questioning enables parents to reply freely, by agreeing in part or whole, denying, ignoring, enlarging or correcting what the helper has said.

Basic exploration

The skills considered already are all relevant to the process of exploring the parents' constructions. They help to provide the parents with a secure relationship in which they have the opportunity to talk and are encouraged to do so, with skilled prompting and empathy. There are, however, some specific points to keep in mind.

Perhaps the most important is that the helper should not be trying to solve problems at this stage. As indicated in relation to the process of helping in Chapter 3, exploration is of major benefit in its own right as it is supportive and allows parents to share their problems. It is also essential before sensible aims can be set and solutions found.

However, there is always a very strong tendency in us all to try to solve people's problems immediately, whether we are professionals or not. People at the beginning of basic counselling training almost invariably try to make suggestions about how to solve a problem within minutes of meeting a person to whom they have been instructed to listen. We seem to do this naturally in spite of the fact that we do not know the person, or all the relevant circumstances. However, if it were that easy, surely the person would have solved the problem him/herself without help. These pressures are increased if we are professionals and have an implicit expert model (see Chapter 3).

What is more, the problems with which we are concerned, involving adaptation to disease and disability, do not have easy solutions. One cannot take away the pain and impotence involved in watching a child suffer. It is impossible to remove the distress of watching a child undergo chemotherapy for months on end, or having to face the limitations of attending a distant hospital for dialysis month after month. You can, however, listen respectfully and allow parents to have these feelings and to express them freely, without trying to take them away. This, in itself, can be extremely helpful and very much valued by parents. What is more, your behaviour might also be a model for them, and indicate strategies to the parents for dealing themselves with their feelings and for supporting their children. Although we do want to find solutions, we have to keep this in check and not feel incompetent when solutions are not immediately forthcoming.

The second point I should like to make is that we should always keep in mind the self-esteem of parents throughout the process of exploration. They must be involved totally, and should discover insights and solutions for themselves, as much as possible. The more they achieve themselves in this way, the more competent and capable they will feel, and the better adapted.

A third point relates to the order in which one conducts the exploration. There is a tendency for us as professionals to lead assessment, but in this context it is important to follow the lead of the parents. They should be free to pursue the issues and problems they consider important in the order they determine and at a pace appropriate to them.

Nevertheless, the helper should be thorough and systematic in the exploration, even if the order is not fixed, and this implies a framework of areas to be explored in turn, if not brought up spontaneously by the parents. Problems vary enormously from family to family, but the categories listed in Chapter 2 as the construct subsystems, form a basis for this exploration. These areas include: the disease/disability, the professionals involved, the child, the self, the spouse, the siblings, other people important to the parents, daily life, and the parents' philosophy. If particular areas are not mentioned by the parents, they should be raised tentatively by the helper so as not to imply that there are problems. They should also not feel forced at such an early stage to discuss issues they find particularly difficult or traumatic.

In raising particular areas, the helper should explain and negotiate what he/she is doing. It is not appropriate to launch into a particular topic without saying why, and without having the person's agreement. 'How is your marriage?' is not a good way to begin to explore the family situation more generally. It may be better to say, 'Sometimes parents in this situation are both so upset that they don't support each other very well. Can I just ask you how you are doing?'. It may even be appropriate to share the whole framework with the parents, and to ask whether you can explore the various areas.

Exploration should be commenced in as open a way as possible, so as not to suggest difficulties or particular directions. However, each problem should be explored as concretely as possible, and it may be helpful to keep the following questions in mind:

➤ What is the general nature of the problem?
➤ How is it manifested specifically?
➤ When did it begin?
➤ What were the circumstances surrounding the onset?
➤ How frequently does the problem arise?
➤ When does it occur?
➤ Where or in what context does it occur?
➤ When and where does it not occur?
➤ Does anything specific trigger the problem?
➤ What are the consequences?
➤ Who is involved in the problem?
➤ How do those involved react?
➤ What do they each think and feel about it?
➤ How do they feel about themselves?
➤ How do they feel about each other?
➤ What are their hypotheses about the reasons for the problem?
➤ What have they tried to do about it?
➤ How successful have their attempts been?

Such exploration takes time, and may last for several sessions. If the major aim of help is to provide support, then the time taken is not relevant, because such exploration will, in itself, be supportive. However, like everything in the relationship, it is important to negotiate explicitly what you do at all stages and for how long.

It has been assumed so far that the exploration will be by discussion in the context of the sessions, and initially this will largely be true. However, more elaborate methods of exploration are available and will be discussed in the next chapter in relation to enabling parents to change. Before finishing this section, it should be pointed out that people do not stop thinking at the end of a meeting with the helper. If it has been productive, they will continue to address the issues during the intervals between meetings. The possibility exists of negotiating with the parents, but not imposing on them, a task for them to do after the session.

One might, for example, ask them to write a few words as a sketch of a particular topic. If the problem is with the self-concept, the person may be asked to do what Kelly (1991) called a self-characterization sketch. This requires them to describe themselves in the third person as though through the eyes of a sympathetic friend. Similarly, they could be asked to write such a sketch about their child or spouse. One parent was asked to write down how she thought her son was feeling about his renal failure, the dialysis and his wait for a kidney. She did this carefully, and we discussed and analysed it at length in the following session. She had found the process of writing in itself informative, but also learnt a great deal from the discussion. What she found was that she needed to check her feelings against those of her son, and she asked him to complete the same task by writing down his feelings. The result was extremely helpful in that this mother realized that her son was not at all as downcast by his experiences as his mother imagined. This in itself relieved her, but it also enabled them to talk, and for the mother to learn that her own sadness had made his adaptation more difficult than it need have been. Different ways of exploring such sketches in relation to the child have been discussed by Davis, Stroud and Green (1989).

The First Meeting

To bring together, illustrate, and clarify what has been said in this chapter so far, I should like to focus upon the first meeting between helper and parents. The fundamental attitudes and basic skills are all relevant to this session, where the aims are to begin to establish the helper–parent relationship and to explore the parents' constructions. Every meeting, including the first, will benefit from preliminary thought so that some idea about what is likely to occur is available to the helper, and any necessary preparations can be made.

Location

Thought needs to be given to the location of the meeting, and my own preference is to visit families at home. The advantage is that they are in their own environment and may, therefore, be less anxious, more in control, less inconvenienced, and have less to do in adapting to the novelty of all aspects of a relatively unknown health care situation. The disadvantage is that the professional has less control over the physical layout (for example, seating arrangements), the degree of privacy, interruptions from the telephone and visitors, and other distractions, such as the television. In practice, however, since most meetings are likely to be in hospitals and clinics, I will, for convenience, assume this here.

The essential requirement of the location is privacy. The likelihood of parents being able to talk about their real feelings and difficulties is remote, to say the least, when for a routine appointment they are confronted with a large clinic room full of a variety of professionals and their students. There should be a room available where there will be no interruptions, either from people walking in or the telephone. A corridor or the bedside in a ward, even with the curtains pulled, are not appropriate venues. Confidentiality is immediately destroyed in such circumstances. Permitting interruptions is disrespectful, as it denies the importance of the people you are with. It is most effective if the helper is alone or, at most, has one other person with them who should be clearly involved.

Ideally the room should be pleasantly decorated without distractions, reasonably spacious, and comfortably lit and heated. More important, however, is that the seating arrangement should be conducive to the interaction. For example, the chairs should be comfortable, of the same height and arranged as naturally as possible. If several members of the family are present, they should be allowed to choose where they sit, although this should usually approximate to a circle. In the case of one person, the best arrangement is to sit at about an angle of 90 degrees to each other, about one-and-a-half metres apart. This is the position naturally adopted by most people sitting together and talking.

Having a desk between the helper and parent contributes little, and may act as a barrier to an open relationship. If required, a desk can be made accessible, by being situated to the side of the helper away from the parent. Using chairs that can be moved easily on castors or can swivel is also useful, as they have the advantage that you can move closer to the parents if they become upset and you want to comfort them by touch.

Greeting

The greeting is important in diffusing initial anxieties and uncertainties that are invariably present when people meet for the first time. To overcome this, one should firstly be punctual, and then welcome them deliberately, warmly and with consideration. It should always involve standing up, looking at each of the people, smiling gently, and acknowledging each of them in turn. Shaking hands is one way of doing this with adults, but if a child is present, she/he should be addressed directly, preferably bending down. One should be aware, however, that children may be particularly anxious of strangers and, therefore, it is important not to be threatening or intrusive. They should not be ignored and should be deliberately involved in the whole conversation.

Part of the greeting process includes introducing the family to the interview room. There are several ways of doing this, ranging from using receptionists to buzzers and tannoy systems. It seems to me, however, that the most respectful way of receiving people is to personally leave the room and to fetch them from wherever they are waiting. I am aware of the practical difficulties this may involve in a busy clinic, but the impression made by doing so is one of caring and respect.

Introduction

It is practical, courteous and respectful to give parents one's name and an indication of one's role as soon as possible. One should never assume that they know. It is equally important to make sure that they have the opportunity to introduce themselves, and that the helper attends individually to each person present. This involves listening carefully and remembering what they say. Since it is a common event that we do not take in names when they are first given, it helps to be unhurried, to relax and to rehearse each name, either by repeating what the person says out loud (for example, 'Hello, Mr Jones') or quietly to one's self. It is patronizing to use first names without requesting explicit permission. Asking children, in particular, for such permission indicates enormous respect, and can enhance the relationship with them.

Initial conversation

The initial conversation, like all other parts of the opening, is an opportunity to reduce preliminary anxieties, to facilitate the subsequent ability to talk openly, and to set in train the formation of an effective relationship. An aspect of this is to be explicit in guiding the parents, for example, in asking them to follow you to your room, giving them permission to sit down and clearly indicating where. The purpose is to minimize uncertainty, and to indicate concern and respect by, for example, allowing them to sit down before yourself.

A second aspect is to initiate a little neutral conversation at the beginning. One might ask about their journey, or comment on the weather. The topic is irrelevant, provided it is natural, spontaneous and genuine. Its purpose is to give the participants the chance to tune into each other's style of conversation, both verbally and non-verbally, and to allow initial impressions to form unhindered by the seriousness of the matters to follow. It is best, therefore, if the conversation is neutral in content, so as not to conflict with what follows. It should also be entirely responsive to the parents, whose lead should be followed, particularly if they spontaneously begin to address their concerns.

Preliminary exploration

If the parents do not immediately bring up the reason for the meeting, the helper should initiate this as the next step. This is usually done by asking an open-ended question, such as, 'Well now, what is it you wanted to discuss?' or 'How can I help you?'. By being open-ended, the question does not prejudice the parents' response, and allows them to tell their story as they please, in any order. Encouragement may be necessary if they hesitate or otherwise minimize their problems.

Once they begin to talk, I think it best not to interfere, but to let them speak for as long as they need, varying from a few sentences to a long and involved description. It may be important to clarify small pieces of information with them on the way but, in general, it is the parents' own constructions that are significant. If they say very little, further open questions may be appropriate. Whatever happens, however, it is important to concentrate upon the story and the way it is being told. Absolute attention, the skills of active listening, prompting, empathy and the points made earlier about exploration, are essential.

An initial contract

It is impossible to completely characterize what occurs next. The helper must simply be responsive to the parents, following what they require. One may, for example, continue with a very detailed exploration of the issues they raise, and we will examine this further in the next chapter. Nevertheless, there will be a point, perhaps when they have given a first description of their concerns, that a contract is formulated. In the case where it is the helper who has initiated the meeting by requesting to see the parents, discussion of the contract may precede the preliminary exploration of the parents' concerns.

Whenever it occurs, what is implied is a negotiation in which the helper and parents reach an explicit agreement about what they are to do together, including if and when to meet again and how frequently.

This involves an exploration of the expectations of both the helper and the parents in order to make an agreement of how to proceed. This is only temporary and is renegotiated at various points thereafter as the situation unfolds and changes, such as at the end of the session when participants need to know what is to happen next.

There is no set way of negotiating the agreement, but one can begin by asking the parents what they know about the helper and the service being provided, and by eliciting their personal expectations. This is important, because it allows the helper to be sure the parents are fully informed and to correct any misconceptions. Without this, the helper is in danger of failing to meet unknown and even unrealistic expectations. For example, it is the point at which one may begin to counter expectations that professionals are all-knowing and all-powerful, and that parents are inferior and have a passive role. The first notions of a partnership may be introduced explicitly here. This can take time and care as in the case of a woman whose child had diabetes and severe behaviour problems. When I asked her for her expectations, it quickly became clear that she thought I would prescribe a medicine that would solve the problems. In fact, our discussion indicated that her unrealistic beliefs about professionals and her poor views of her own competence were significant causes of the problems in the child, so that the negotiation became a crucial part of handling the whole problem.

Ending

If the major aims are to provide support, and the problems are not minor, little more can be expected of a first meeting than establishing the helper–parent relationship, exploring at least initially the problems presented by the parents and negotiating a contract. If these have been achieved, then a great deal has been done to lay the foundations of a very supportive long-term relationship. However, finishing the meeting is difficult and should be done well. It is useful, therefore, to negotiate clearly at the outset how much time there is together, and to try to stick to this. The duration can vary, but my own inclination is to set aside 50 to 60 minutes.

It is important, therefore, to monitor the time unobtrusively, and to give about a ten-minute warning of the end of the session. This allows the parents and helpers to orientate themselves, to draw together and summarize what has happened, to agree what to do next and to finish. A warning enables people to compose themselves if they have been upset, but care should be taken to check whether they are sufficiently recovered to be able to cope with their journey home. A quiet room, and perhaps a drink, may be provided for those needing time to settle down. Leave should be taken simply, courteously and quickly, for example, by standing up, allowing the parents to rise, and then escorting them to the door.

Occasionally, parents introduce a new and perhaps urgent problem at the very end. If so, it must be acknowledged, but it should be tactfully put off until the beginning of the next meeting. It would be impossible to find sudden solutions at such a late stage to problems that have not been adequately explored. This can be shared with the parents, who must also accept, for example, that you have other people waiting. This may make you feel as though you are failing the parents, but it is important to keep in mind that it is not the helper's role to solve all problems, but to help people to solve them themselves. They may also learn to use the time of future sessions better.

Note-taking

I try not to take notes during a session, as it is impossible to both write and relate to people in the responsive and skilled way advocated here. It also makes the conversation disjointed and makes it difficult for the parents to know when they can talk. If there is the need to note down information, then I tend to seek the parent's permission or to explain why before doing so.

The preferable course is to make notes when the session has ended. People have their own ways of doing this, but it is important to make a short summary of what transpired, what information is important to remember, and what was agreed. It is useful to make a clear list of hypotheses or feelings that have occurred during the session, and to make a note of any plans for subsequent meetings. These can be read before the next time, so as to orientate the helper and to prepare for and initiate the next session appropriately.

Case Example

A mother and father met their helper, in this case a health visitor. They came with their eight-year-old son, who was becoming more and more resistant to having his routine blood tests at the clinic. He had begun to scream and struggle, and had to be held down firmly. This was distressing to all concerned and made obtaining a sample very difficult.

Together they explored the problem over a couple of sessions, and found that there was a more general relationship problem between the mother and son. The helper constantly engaged the son in the discussion with the parents. Together the helper and the family formulated an explanation that involved mother's extreme distress at the onset of the disease, powerful worries about her only son dying, and a desperate desire to take the disease away. Added to this she could not stand him being hurt in any way. It was thought that it was mother's tension that exaggerated her son's fears, which were further fuelled by his parents' failure to discuss anything about his illness with him. They did not prepare him for clinic visits and the necessary tests in any way.

The mother's worries and difficulties in adapting to the disease were the major subject of several further sessions with the health visitor. In addition to this, however, they discussed how to handle the son's blood tests. What was agreed, was that mother should find opportunities to be with him in the hope of being able to get him to talk about his illness and resistance. She determined for herself that she had to find out what he was thinking and feeling. She decided that she had to stop scolding and trying to persuade him to think and act differently, and rather that she needed to listen to what he had to say and to respect and accept his views, without trying to change them.

These strategies in themselves led to enormous improvements in both the child and mother, and the relationship between them. She began to realize that he had accepted the illness very well and was minimizing the effects and limitations on him. She realized that it was her anxieties and worries that made him react negatively, and she began to relax and to enjoy her son for himself, trying to put aside the disease problems.

The impetus for change had occurred, and the parents were able to relate to the child in a much more open way; allowing him to talk and explore and to share in decisions, also sharing with him all information in an open way. This included telling him well in advance when clinic appointments were due. They were honest about the need for the blood tests. With advice from the health visitor, they helped him to relax himself, and to breathe deeply as a means of controlling his fear. They helped him work out a distraction strategy by which he said 'Stop!' to himself whenever he became frightened. At the same time, he would visualize scenes from his favourite television programme. They obtained a syringe that he was able to examine and use on a teddybear. Perhaps more important, they put him in control, allowing him to decide whether he needed the test and whether he would allow it to happen. His eventual success was rewarded profusely by praise from all concerned and a trip to the cinema was arranged.

One of the mother's comments to the health visitor by way of evaluation was: 'We hadn't learned to treat him (her son) properly. What we did in the end was to listen to him, like you listen to us and him, and we helped him succeed himself, without us trying to solve things for him'.

Concluding Remarks

What we have considered here are basic characteristics and skills needed by helpers to provide first class support for parents facing the stress and distress of having a child with a chronic disease or disability. For me, these are qualities essential to establishing a trusting working partnership with parents, so as to provide them with someone to whom they can talk about their difficulties. These characteristics, in themselves, are of benefit to parents, most of whom will feel much better about themselves and their whole situation as a result, and for some this will be sufficient. However, although most important, establishing a relationship and initial exploration of their concerns is often only the beginning of the process of helping which continues, as described in the previous chapter, with the aim of enabling parents to change the ways they construe their situation. This means helping them to develop models that are the most useful to them in setting goals and then formulating plans to achieve them. The skills described so far are fundamental to the whole process, but there are also specific ways of helping people change, and these will be considered in the next chapter.

Summary

❑ It is proposed that there are fundamental attitudes that, if exhibited by the helper and perceived by the parents, will be beneficial to families. These include:

- respect or holding parents and children in esteem;
- humility or realistic acceptance of oneself;
- genuineness or sincere openness to experience without distortion;
- empathy or trying to understand the world from the other's viewpoint;
- quiet enthusiasm involving willingness and pleasure in helping.

❑ Such attitudes must be expressed in all aspects of the helper's behaviour, but they can be demonstrated and made effective by a set of skills basic to helping.

❑ These are the skills of attending, active listening, prompting, empathic responding and basic exploration.

❑ These attitudes and skills are the essential ingredients of helping in that they are prerequisites of the whole process, but especially because they serve to establish the relationship with the parents and enable understanding of their problems.

— continued —

❏ They are the first tasks in the process of helping and can be considered the most important in fostering parental self-esteem and self-efficacy, and a thorough understanding of the situations they confront.

❏ Exploration involves problem understanding and not the immediate search for solutions. It should be responsive to the lead and pace of the parents, but broad and thorough.

❏ Specific problems should be explored concretely and in depth in relation to their nature, time sequence, context, consequences and origins or causes. The feelings and behaviour of those involved, and the strategies already attempted should also be examined.

❏ All meetings with the family, and particularly the first, should be planned and prepared carefully.

❏ The location is important, and should enable privacy with no interruptions or distractions. Appropriate and comfortable seating arrangements should be provided.

❏ Consideration should be given to greeting, introduction and initial neutral conversation to enable parents and children to relax and adapt to the new and potentially stressful situation.

❏ The first session will involve preliminary exploration of the situation/problems, and negotiation of an initial contract so that there is explicit agreement about what is to occur in both the present and future meetings.

❏ Finishing is difficult, but is helped by explicit negotiation of the time available at the very beginning, and a warning toward the end.

❏ This warning gives time for participants to compose themselves after experiencing any emotional distress, and it provides a little time for the helper to respond to difficult issues that are occasionally raised spontaneously in the last few minutes.

5

Helping Parents Change

Being told the news of a serious or chronic disease is a point at which parents are forced to change (as discussed in Chapter 2). The qualities and skills involved in breaking bad news include those discussed in the last chapter as well as a range of other skills to be considered here. As a preface to this discussion, however, I should like to look at breaking bad news in some depth.

Breaking Bad News

The disclosure of the diagnosis is important to consider for a number of reasons:

- It happens at least once to all families in the context of chronic disease. However, it might occur many times. Parents may learn initially of a disease involving their child's kidneys. They may then be told that the kidneys have failed. There may later follow difficulties with dialysis, or the news that a transplant has been unsuccessful. Later still they may be told that the child has little time to live, or that he/she does not want to continue with treatment.
- It is a traumatic event for the family, even in cases where the professional may think the problem trivial. For example, parents may be devastated by the news of a relatively small hearing loss.
- The disclosure is the beginning of the adaptation process. The way in which it is done may affect the provision of all subsequent help, and will certainly influence the speed, if not the extent, to which the parents develop coping strategies. If done well, for example, it may enhance the parent–professional relationship ever after. It is, however, frequently done badly, and increases parental distress unnecessarily. For example, a mother was so completely staggered by the information that her daughter had to have further surgery, that she took in no other details, including what was to be done or why. She conjured up images of malignancies, when in reality the operation was minor. The clinician had given this information, but had not allowed time for her to recover from her initial shock before

giving her the details. The reasons for such problems are many, but include the anxieties of the clinicians involved, lack of understanding of the processes of communication and adaptation, and inadequate training and skills. The evidence is that although guidelines have been available for several years on how to disclose the diagnosis skilfully, there has been little improvement in how it is done.

- All professionals are involved and have to do it sometime (for example, in giving a test result), even if only in going over what the paediatrician said originally so as to help parents fully understand. For example, one of my colleagues, acting as a parent adviser, had to tell the parents of their son's heart condition, because they had not understood the seriousness or the details of what they had been told at a regional centre.

I will provide a list of points to be considered in three stages (preparation, consultation and ending). These should be considered in the context of all that has gone before, including the notions of partnership, the fundamental qualities and core skills of helping and the helping process.

Preparation

The person breaking the news should have time to prepare as carefully as possible before actually meeting the parents, and the following points should be considered:

Who should give the information? This should preferably be someone who knows the parents, and has appropriate communication skills and relevant knowledge. No other staff should be present unless they have a clear role, and their presence is explained or negotiated with the parents.

To whom should the information be given? Parents usually want to be told together, and prefer their baby to be present if it is a congenital problem identified at birth. For older children, however, parents may want to decide what and how to tell the child. In the absence of one parent, alternative support (by a friend, relative or staff member) should be arranged before the consultation, to be available to the parent once the diagnosis has been given.

What should be said? All relevant information should be available if necessary, but decisions should be made about what parents should be told, the priorities, the order in which to give it, and the terminology to be used. Only what is absolutely essential should be given at this stage, unless specifically requested by the parents, as the shock will inhibit both their understanding and retention.

Where should they be told? The most appropriate venue should be selected, but privacy is the essential factor. Arrangements should be made to avoid all interruptions, including the telephone. Tissues should be available, and chairs positioned appropriately to enable physical comfort to be given if necessary.

Allow plenty of time.

The consultation

Many of the points made in the last chapter about the first meeting between helper and parents are relevant here, particularly to do with greeting the parents, making introductions and engaging in brief neutral conversation. No two meetings are ever the same, but as a general guide, the following may be considered:

Be attentive. The person giving the news should be closely aware of the parents the whole time, and responsive to their mood and behaviour.

Respond appropriately. The communicator should be as relaxed and unhurried as possible, being gentle, quiet, slow and clear in all verbal and non-verbal behaviour. Your mood should not clash with that of the parents.

Explain. The reason for the consultation should be explained clearly and precisely.

Follow the parents. If the parents take the lead at this point or at any other time in the interview, the professional should follow.

Determine what they know. Find out what the parents already know, think and feel about the problem. They may have accurate or inaccurate information from many sources, and will almost certainly have fears. Good prior communication will certainly have forewarned the parents of the possibility of bad news.

Provide appropriate information. What parents say will determine the information to be provided. The more related the information is to their existing beliefs or knowledge, the more meaningful it will be. However, all information should be as simple, clear and brief as possible at this stage; perhaps just the diagnosis, if this is meaningful to parents. Any unavoidable technical terms should be explained. Whatever is said should be honest, accurate and balanced, neither falsely reassuring nor unduly negative. I frequently hear physicians saying in relation to informing people about the nearness of their death, 'You must not take hope away'. When questioned, they often imply that they would blur the truth to be kind. To me, this is dishonest and unacceptable. If there is no hope of survival, it is disrespectful to imply otherwise. If by not removing hope, they imply offering emotional support, comfort and practical help to ease the path ahead, then I agree entirely.

Pause. After providing the diagnosis, one should leave a long pause to allow the parents to respond, whether with silence, stunned shock, confusion, incomprehension, distress or anger. The informant should be prepared for a range of reactions, and, potentially, extreme emotion will be expressed. Parents might express incomprehension; they might try to deny what has been said; they may be angry with themselves or the staff; they may cry quietly, or weep uncontrollably. Whatever happens, no attempt should be made to stop it. It should be accepted as natural and an important part of the parents' current coping strategies. Parents should be allowed to take control and determine what occurs subsequently, while the helper listens sensitively and follows their lead. Their feelings, justified or not, should be accepted without argument or criticism at this stage.

Answer all questions. Do so clearly and honestly, admitting ignorance or uncertainty.

Be empathic. Enquire about the parents' feelings and thoughts if they do not give them spontaneously. Accept their views as valid for them at that moment, although they may only be temporary hypotheses.

Comfort. Do so as necessary. You may touch the parents if this is not intrusive.

Do not hide your feelings. Honest expressions of the professional's feelings (for example, sadness or anxiety) are valued by parents as indicating genuine care and humanity.

Explore particular questions. This may be necessary, once the parents have reacted initially. However, they should not be overloaded; spending a little time in silence with them may be valued, although they will fill the gap if uncomfortable.

Ending

At some point the session must end, even though it may feel difficult to finish.

Negotiate the end. Give a few minutes warning of your intention to finish. Seek the parents' agreement and do not hurry.

Summarize. Briefly summarize what has been said and attempt to check the parents' understanding. Repetition of the main information is useful.

Agree on a general plan. You should plan together what is to happen next. This should include an early follow-up appointment to 1) demonstrate care and support; 2) allow information to be repeated, checked and clarified; 3) add further information; and 4) provide answers to the many questions the parents will inevitably have.

Negotiate immediate action. Before finishing, the parents should be allowed to decide what they want to do immediately, such as sitting alone for a while, perhaps with a drink; sitting with another professional such as a nurse; or leaving for the comfort and security of their own home.

Allow time for yourself to relax. You may need to be alone or with a colleague when the parents leave.

Liaise with other staff as necessary.

Challenging Skills

If the disclosure interview is done well, parents will have been changed in ways that have hurt them (this cannot be avoided), but their pain will not have been increased unnecessarily. They will have the beginnings of an understanding of the disease, will not have been undermined, and will know there is good professional support available to them. This meets several of the aims of helping listed in Chapter 3.

Many of the aims and objectives described earlier involve the facilitation of change. In general, this means changes to the construct system that parents have for anticipating all aspects of their world. This, in turn, results in changes to the ways in which they adapt to or solve the problems facing them.

As said earlier, such changes may result simply from the opportunity to explore the situation with someone who is skilled in communicating and has the qualities described in the last chapter. If parents are aware of being valued, their self-esteem may increase, as well as their ability to cope.

However, not all change occurs as easily, and the helper may have to adopt a variety of skills and strategies to facilitate the process. In general, this involves the helper in deriving an accurate picture of the world as seen through the eyes of the parents, whilst at the same time evaluating its adequacy in enabling the parent to adapt. To do this, the helper has to compare the parent's model with alternatives derived from the helper's own constructions. The advantage of this is that the helper is less involved in the problem and potentially more objective.

Such comparison may lead the helper to conclude, for example, that the parents are very unclear about their own role in the cause of the disease, or have misconceptions about the prognosis. They may not understand the behaviour of the child and not know what to do about behaviour problems. They may construe their own parents as unhelpful, or the helper may see them as very anxious. In short, the parents may have any number of difficulties (as illustrated in Chapter 2), either acknowledged by them or not.

The tasks of the helper are to enable parents to see the difficulties clearly and to stimulate them to change in order to adopt a more effective model. The skills to do this are the subject of this chapter, and are called *challenging skills* (Egan, 1982).

The word challenge is used respectfully to acknowledge the parents' active role in determining change. It implies a process of presenting them with, or offering, a new or alternative perspective for their consideration. Whatever the helper's view, the parents are at liberty to adopt, discuss, or reject the model offered. I will describe a number of major strategies for challenging parents, but before I do, it is worth noting some common principles.

- ➤ Challenging should preferably occur within a mutually trusting relationship. Because challenges are by nature threatening and potentially hurtful, without such trust parents may not listen to what the helper has to say.
- ➤ The reason for challenges should be clear and for the parents' benefit.
- ➤ They should be expressed in words parents can understand.
- ➤ They should be as concise as possible. Parents will lose attention during long monologues and they are difficult to follow.
- ➤ Challenges should be concrete and specific.
- ➤ They should be positive, directed at strengths not weaknesses.
- ➤ They should be invitational and tentative, hypotheses to be tested, not factual matters to be automatically accepted.

Giving information

What we have illustrated already, and perhaps the most common way of challenging people to change, is by giving them new information.

As professionals we do this constantly, in providing a diagnosis, giving a test result or prescribing a treatment. In each case, new information is presented and it is usually assumed that the parent will take it in, accept it and change the way they construe the situation. However, unless we communicate well, they may not understand the information, they may not agree, they may attempt to invalidate it, or they may forget much of it. This is frequently what happens, and the result is that the possibility of change is reduced (see Davis and Fallowfield, 1991b).

Since challenging parents with information is so important to their adaptation, it should be done skilfully by all professionals. The general process is as follows:

1. *Begin with what they know already.* The first step in giving information is an enquiry stage to determine the parents' prior knowledge and manner of communication. It is difficult to give information appropriately without this – try giving directions to someone at the other end of a telephone without first establishing where they are! Such enquiry is, of course, a prerequisite of all helping, and is what exploration is all about, as described in the last chapter. If it is done carefully, it makes the whole process easier. For example, one young registrar told me of his hesitation in approaching a couple to inform them of what was thought to be the imminent death of their son on a cardiac unit. With considerable trepidation, he met the parents in private and began by carefully asking them about their fears and expectations. They replied in a resigned way that, although no one had talked to them about it, they knew that he had little time to live. They also felt they could face this prospect, because their son had already talked to them about it himself.

2. *Present the information.* After appropriate enquiry and learning where to begin, the necessary information can be presented so as to maximize the parents' comprehension and recall. The words used should be as understandable and simple as possible. Only necessary information should be given, and this in small amounts paced by the parents. It should be structured, if possible, into clear categories, beginning with an explicit outline of the structure. For example, information about a disease may be structured in terms of: 1) diagnosis; 2) underlying pathology; 3) causes; 4) prognosis; and 5) treatment. Repetition also aids recall, as does an indication of the relative importance of particular information.

3. *Check the result.* This is occurring all the time in the sense that the information-giver monitors the listener constantly while talking. How-

ever, once all the information has been presented, it is important to determine the effect; that is, to check what the parents now know, whether they are clear or have any misunderstandings, and how they feel about it. This can be done by inviting the parents to ask questions, but also by asking questions of them and by discussion. If there are problems, then one goes through the process again by presenting the information in a more accessible way and again checking the result. It is certainly clear in my experience that parents need to go over the details of a serious diagnosis many times in the early days following disclosure, and only gradually acquire an overall model of the problem.

4. *Ensure retention.* This whole process will begin to ensure that parents remember the information, but it is always important to find ways of helping this to occur, where possible. This might include: writing down what has been said; giving pamphlets; referring them to further reading; or recording the conversation on audiotape so that the parents can take it home and listen to it at their leisure, and even share it with other relatives and friends (see, for example, Hogbin and Fallowfield, 1989).

Summarizing

Another way of gently challenging parents to change their models, both as an adjunct to giving information or on its own, is to offer them a summary of what has occurred in the interaction between the helper and parents. This may clarify and simplify information given and may provide some repetition to enhance retention of the facts.

When summaries are used to explore parents' models or understanding of their problems, they serve the purpose of checking the accuracy of the helper's developing model, they indicate empathy, they show that helpers are listening carefully, and they may present a clear overview that has not been previously available to parents. Summaries are, therefore, gently challenging in that they may stimulate insight, understanding and a change in perspective.

Summarizing statements should be as brief as possible, but accurate and clear. The following summary was offered by a health visitor: 'So! You think there are a number of possible reasons for why Ian (the son) gets so angry. It's possibly because he's tired and run down, or frightened of what is going to happen at the hospital, or because you're tense and somehow transmit your feelings, making him less secure'. In response, the mother hesitated, as though thinking, then said, 'Well . . . that's right . . . but it's probably more to do with me than him. I get so tense before we go (to hospital) . . . In fact, exactly the same happens before John (the estranged father) comes round. Ian always plays up, because I get so snappy'. This not only reflects the mother's developing realization of her role in the child's problem, but it was also the first time she had brought her ex-husband into the conversation. The helper's summary meets the criteria for challenging listed earlier in being relatively short, accurate, specific and concrete, and with the purpose of helping the mother's clarity. It was also given in a tentative way, partly indicated by 'So! You think . . .', and partly by the questioning tone of voice.

Like all challenges, summarizing should not be over-used. However, it is a particularly useful way of: beginning new sessions; stimulating the conversation when it is flagging or feels stuck; drawing together scattered thoughts and feelings; prompting further exploration; and even closing a particular issue.

Self-disclosure

It is often assumed that one should not discuss one's personal life when helping others because such self-disclosure can be intrusive, and distracts attention from the parents as the focus of the intervention. However, if used sparingly, it can be advantageous in challenging parents to change by presenting a different view. This may be done, for example, by indicating similarity and implying that the parents are not so strange or different from other people (for example, 'I'm the same. I always get anxious when I go to the doctor, even when there's no major problem'). Alternatively, self-disclosure can challenge by presenting a direct contrast. In response to a mother having difficulty coping with the demands of her children to whom she felt she had to be perfect, a counsellor said, 'I try to meet all their demands, but my children just laugh at my forgetfulness!'.

The intention is to help the parent change, but it is also a useful way of showing empathy, humility and genuineness, thereby fostering the parent–helper relationship. It can serve to indicate that the helper is not superhuman. This can break down a potential barrier to communication and allow parents to talk more openly. Whatever the reason for using this kind of challenge, the general principles of being tentative, concise, positive and specific as well as operating within a good working relationship, are as relevant as ever. It is important to ensure, however, that there are good reasons for doing this, and that one does not just need to talk about oneself or to impress.

Advanced empathy

We have already discussed empathy – both as a general attitude of attempting to understand the worldview of the parents and as a basic skill of reflecting back their meaning. This aids change by indicating respect and by presenting to parents their model as clearly as possible.

Advanced empathy, on the other hand, takes this a stage further by presenting parents with what they have not said, but probably meant. When listening carefully, the helper may become aware of all kinds of feelings, constructions and implications that the parents have not stated, or even quite grasped. For example, whilst a mother talked lightly about the lack of practical support from her husband in looking after their daughter with severe osteopetrosis, the helper began to get the impression that there was a deep resentment involved. Another mother seemed to be very negative about her daughter, who was seriously ill with renal disease, after a transplant rejection and difficulties with dialysis. The helper gently commented on what appeared to be a negative attitude, and suggested that she might be feeling very angry about the possibility of losing her daughter. Although staggered by this suggestion, the mother went on to talk about her anger, to explore how upset she felt about manifesting such feelings in relation to her daughter, and to begin to talk to her daughter about her feelings, to the benefit of them both.

The technique of advanced empathy is used to present the implications of their models to parents, with the intention of helping them to change to clearer and even totally different views of their situations. If successful, the person will become aware of something that they could not face previously, had not grasped, or had misinterpreted. 'Perhaps you're getting upset with your son, when actually you're angry about your own inability to help him' is an example of this skill, addressed to a father who could not enjoy interacting with his son who had arthritis. Another example of advanced empathy is the following statement made to a mother who was trying to decide how to stop her son (with a mild hemiplegia) from playing football, his passion, before he was dropped from the team. Although the mother had only talked about the child, the teacher said, 'But what is really upsetting is your own feeling of being unable to protect him any longer'.

The fact that in both cases the parents immediately began to weep is an indication of the power of this skill. It stimulated open expression of their feelings, and subsequent discussion that was very productive. Nevertheless, such statements are potentially very threatening to parents and that is why they were only attempted within a secure relationship and were made in a very gentle, invitational way. Although the effect was to move the parents and to help them change, such skills also enhanced the relationship with the helpers, who were seen as caring, highly understanding and not judgemental. Such power does necessitate careful consideration of why one should attempt advanced empathy and when.

Immediacy

Immediacy, or you–me talk, is an important challenging skill, and refers to the ability to talk about what is occurring in the immediate helping situation between the helper and parents, or in their relationship generally. Although this is an important aspect of working in partnership, it is something that occurs infrequently except in very intimate relationships or in anger. We rarely express our feelings for each other verbally, or attempt to analyse our relationship, even though it is a vital component of a deep and effective partnership. Consider the difficulties of talking to colleagues about your feelings for them, whether positive or negative, or theirs for you. We have difficulty and embarrassment in complimenting others enthusiastically, and even more problems in talking about their inadequacies or their mistakes, as this appears to threaten our relationship. Most teams with whom I have ever worked have at least one member who is resented by the rest for incompetence or lack of motivation, yet rarely is this addressed effectively.

If one is to work closely with others, either in a professional team or as a helper, then the skills of immediacy are essential – both as a means of enhancing the relationship and as a way of helping people with problems. Parents may bring to the relationship with the helper the same difficulties they have in relating to other people in their lives. Discussion of this, therefore, can help them to see these problems more clearly, and to change. However, this is again a powerful and potentially very threatening strategy, and should certainly be done with careful consideration of the criteria of challenging (see page 83).

As an illustration, I worked for several weeks with a mother whose child had severe gut problems and serious developmental delay, which she appeared to be denying. She had a dominant manner that strained our relationship. She made me feel irritated and alienated by being very condescending. This seemed to have a bearing on more general interpersonal problems with her husband, her children, the paediatric staff and other parents on the ward. Once I felt that our relationship was sufficiently secure, I addressed these problems by asking her how she felt about our sessions. This elicited somewhat negative comments. I responded by asking if she had gained anything at all, whereupon she became much more positive. I then tentatively asked her how I might have felt about her original negative comments, and she admitted they may have been hurtful. This allowed us to look at the contradiction between the negative comments and her more positive feelings, and then to consider if this was a general tendency that might alienate people around her. My enquiry was positive and not motivated by personal hurt. I wanted to minimize the extent to which she felt attacked. I was concerned about damaging our relationship, but was aware of the enormous potential gains, which in this case were attained. She explored her feelings for, and specific behaviour towards, other people and as a result was able to improve her relationship with significant people in her life.

Confrontation

I have looked at challenges in order of increasing threat and therefore difficulty of use. The last to be mentioned and the most difficult is confrontation. This involves directly challenging parents by confronting them with a completely different model of the problem, in contradiction to their own. Here, the helper is stepping outside of the parents' own model and contrasting it with what the helper thinks. Of all we have discussed, this comes nearest to the helper being overtly judgemental.

One might confront discrepancies, distortions or self-defeating beliefs. For example, one might challenge a parent with the discrepancy that although she has agreed a course of action (for example, a drug regime) with the GP, she has consistently failed to carry it out. Similarly, one might have to point out that although a couple frequently promise their children to be home early from their business, they rarely keep their promise. It may be important to confront a parent's belief that his/her child is coping in a particular school, when it is clear that this is not true. It may also be appropriate to challenge self-defeating attitudes of parents, believing, for example, that they always have to be perfect or do the right thing. This happened when a mother thought she was completely useless simply because she failed to notice the early onset of her daughter's disease. These are but a few of the situations in which it may be valuable to use confrontation.

All such situations are potentially extremely embarrassing and threatening to parents, and can be seen as deliberate attacks if done poorly. The intention is not to attack, but to question in a way that enables the person to see the discrepancy or distortion, and develop a new perspective. Caricaturing this a little, confronting a father on one's very first meeting with, 'I see you have completely failed to tell your son about his cancer' may serve only to obtain an angry barrage of abuse and a hasty exit. Taking care to follow the guidelines listed earlier about challenging in general may improve the situation considerably.

In a real situation, this problem arose because a child was close to death and seemed to know it. However, the father had trouble facing it, and refused to tell or allow the child to be told. The effects were numerous, but led to the family having difficulties in communicating with and deriving comfort from each other, both in the immediate situation and possibly for the long-term (that is, after the child's death). The ward psychologist, therefore, confronted the father, as she had the closest relationship with him. She raised the issue by saying, 'You have a wonderful open relationship with your son, but I have the feeling there's a conflict. I think he knows he has little time to live and would like to be able to talk about it with you'. Although the father was very upset, he listened to what she had to say, and began to talk about it for the first time. As a result, they agreed on a tentative plan of approaching the child in a way that would allow him to talk. This was done by the father going to his son on his own and sitting quietly with him. As the result of discussion with the psychologist, the father did not force the conversation along, but touched his son gently and asked how he was feeling. He listened carefully to the reply and followed up what he said with further prompts. This gradually led to his son talking about the future, and the father started to weep quietly. The boy took his hand and indicated that they did not have long together. They both wept and held each other. This event was, needless to say, extremely distressing for the father, but it was a relief to him eventually, as it was for the child and the rest of the family.

This was a clear confrontation by the helper, but it worked because there was a sufficiently strong relationship and because the manner of the psychologist was tentative, gentle and questioning. She began with reference to the strength of the father, was very clear and specific, was motivated by concern for the family, and provided the opportunity to explore the problem. It was done with respect, giving him every opportunity to talk, and listening carefully. It was done without accusation, but as a hypothesis to be explored together to see the truth of the matter, allowing disagreement as a legitimate possibility.

More General Strategies: Construct Theory

I have described basic skills for exploring the constructions that parents have and for helping them to change, no matter what the problem area. There are, however, many other more specialized and elaborate techniques that may be helpful in this process, and these may be discovered by reading about any of the different schools of professional counselling. Particularly worth effort are the problem management approach of Egan (1982), the work of Ellis (for example, in Dryden, 1990), and Kelly (for example, in Fransella and Dalton, 1990).

Rather than being prescriptive, I should like to end this chapter by presenting a general model, derived from construct theory (described in Chapter 2). This guide should enable helpers to invent ways of helping parents to develop and test alternative perspectives in order to change. The analogy throughout this discussion is that the helper and parents act in their partnership like *experimental scientists*, formulating competing hypotheses and testing them to evaluate their validity and utility in dealing with problems.

Sharing the model

If one is truly to operate in partnership with parents, then a general way to help them explore and change begins by sharing with them the model of help that the helper is using. This might involve sharing any aspect of the models described in this book so far, including the model of partnership and the aims, process, and skills of helping. I, personally, have no hesitation in explaining and describing what I think I am doing. However, here I am specifically referring to the model of personal constructs (introduced in Chapter 2). The relevant aspects include the notions that:

- we all construe the world differently;
- there are always alternative ways of looking at events;
- each is like a hypothesis derived from a personal theory;
- they are not written in tablets of stone;
- we could usefully act as scientists to test them as best we can;
- we should evaluate the results, and possibly change the hypotheses.

Explicitly sharing this model with the parents forms the basis of facilitating change. It includes helping parents to see that none of their views are absolute. Rather, they are like templates or models that are more or less accurate or useful, and there may be alternatives. Illustrations may help parents to grasp this. For example, the parents of a child with a serious brain injury construed his hand-flapping behaviour as embarrassing, repetitive and meaningless. Having noticed, however, that it only occurred when he was happy and excited and looking at them, they came to see it as his first real way of communicating with them, and this signalled a break-through.

An adolescent boy with diabetes was viewed by his father as uncommunicative, unruly, rude and disobedient. The family friends across the road construed him as polite, helpful, extremely competent and very good company. His teacher saw him as clever, but lazy and disruptive. The other boys saw him as extremely funny and creative, and various girls saw him as very handsome and rather cool. He, however, construed himself as shy, anxious of other people, not at all competent, and made very much worse by his illness.

The points to learn here include not only that people act differently in different situations, but that the same behaviour may be construed completely differently, depending upon the model or template being used by the perceiver. A person's constructions are not direct reflections of reality, but are hypotheses that may be more or less valid in anticipating future events. Different models are, therefore, of different value in helping adaptation.

Once parents (or children for that matter) have understood the general theory, they can be helped to use it. The steps in the process need to be shared and understood, including: 1) clearly identifying the constructs or hypotheses they use; 2) carefully listing all the alternatives; 3) testing them systematically; and 4) evaluating the results. I will illustrate the process below with real case examples. I will also focus upon the consideration of causal constructions, because this is important in trying to understand and solve problems. However, this is not to imply that all hypotheses must relate to causes.

Formulating hypotheses

A mother, whose eight-year-old son, Peter, had asthma, with frequent and serious episodes, worked with me to look at a complex of social and family difficulties. Just one of the issues with which she was concerned was Peter's difficult behaviour. We explored her general constructions of him by completing a child characterization sketch as described in Chapter 2. This involved her giving a detailed description of her son, recorded on a cassette recorder. (She could have done it in writing just as easily.) We played it back together and made a list of the main attributes she used in her description. Her main constructions appeared to be that he was disobedient, angry, aggressive, difficult to control and unhappy. We then investigated the specific behaviour problems by listing each difficult situation identified by his mother using the so-called ABC model (see, for example, Herbert, 1988). In this model, A refers to the antecedents of each behaviour problem, including the places, times, people involved and the triggers. B refers to a detailed description of the actual behaviour, including its frequency; and C refers to the consequences, such as how the mother responded. We also explored more generally what she thought caused the problems.

Although she kept saying that she did not understand why Peter acted as he did, what she learned was that she had a whole series of possible explanations, without knowing which was right. We therefore spent some time generating and writing down the list of possible hypotheses. She wrote:

- *'He is just a horrible person.'*
- *'It is because of his asthma.'*
- *'Because of his fears of not being able to breathe and possibly dying.'*
- *'Because of diet (for example, vast quantities of tomato ketchup).'*
- *'Too much attention.'*
- *'Getting everything he wants with no consistent demands made on him.'*
- *'His father is too lenient with him.'*
- *'Because of his resentments about being ill.'*
- *'Because of my anxieties about him and the illness.'*

These are short statements referring to the essence of the explanations generated by the mother, who described them at greater length in our session. It is interesting to note, however, that she felt much better after simply formulating this list; she described a sense of achievement. Although she had half grasped all these explanations at different times, she had done so in a way that was tinged with panic, and had never explored them systematically or calmly.

In a second case, a father of a child with end-stage renal failure came to discuss his daughter's avoidance of and coldness towards him. Although this was specifically considered, much of the discussion focused upon the father's poor opinion of himself and his own unhappiness. These were seen as major problems and at least a partial explanation for him alienating people. Again we explored widely all the areas of his construct system and included a self-characterization sketch. When we considered the explanations for his depression and low self-esteem, the following list was generated:

- *'I can't cure her disease.'*
- *'I am a born worrier.'*
- *'I focus on the negative, never acknowledging what I do well.'*
- *'My wife puts me down because I don't trust her to do things herself.'*
- *'Everyone else seems so competent and confident, which makes me think I am odd.'*
- *'I don't understand the children and unintentionally upset them.'*
- *'I never solve the problems we have as a family.'*
- *'I'm afraid my daughter might die.'*
- *'No one ever praises me; they just criticize.'*
- *'I worry about being useless, and as a result I don't trust others.'*

Testing the hypotheses

Having made an exhaustive list of possible explanations, the next step is to test them. The question is which of these hypotheses, if any, have useful explanatory value, in terms of suggesting what to do about the problems identified. The helper can share with the parents the task of experimenting together, trying to find ways to test the hypotheses so as to accept, reject or modify them, and gain a usable explanation.

Ways of testing hypotheses are endless, limited only by the imagination of the helper and parents. As in science, the design of an experiment is a creative process, and there are no set methods. However, possible directions can be outlined.

Discussion with the helper. The simplest way of testing hypotheses is by detailed discussion between the parent and helper. They may take each hypothesis in turn and question the evidence for and against it. Where possible, the parents should lead the debate, but the helper can contribute as necessary.

To take one of the examples above, the statement that the child's difficult behaviour followed directly from having asthma was questioned. This mother said that other women with whom she talked said their children with asthma were difficult, but it appeared that the only mothers she knew well attended a group for difficult children. I questioned whether she talked to mothers at the outpatient clinic and, being rather shy, she did not. However, she had noticed that her son was usually the only child being difficult. She then remembered that two of her cousins had had asthma as children. This clearly refuted the hypothesis as they had always been 'lovely' children and she adored them. Any remaining doubt, arising from the fact that as a child she might not have been aware of them being difficult, was removed by me saying that I saw a whole range of personalities in children with asthma.

Similarly, the hypothesis about him being naturally horrible was refuted by noting the occasions on which he demonstrated good feelings for others. In particular, he seemed to care deeply about his younger sister, protecting her closely. The discussion, however, gave indications that the problem may relate more to the mother's own feelings (the last hypothesis in the list), in that she always expected him to be difficult and construed everything he did negatively. The other hypotheses were similarly explored, initially by discussion and then by other means.

Discussion with others. Another way to test formulated hypotheses is for the parent to discuss them with other professionals, family members or friends. The helper and parent may agree that they do not have the knowledge to test all the hypotheses, and therefore try to think who might. The mother we have just been discussing took the initiative of approaching the dietician for evidence about the effects of food on behaviour. The father, mentioned previously, who construed everyone but himself as confident, sampled a number of friends to ask them how they felt in certain situations, and was amazed to find how frequently they hid embarrassment and anxieties.

An important advantage for parents in this situation is that they are more likely to feel in control, particularly with other professionals. The parent is not just asking for explanations; she/he has done much of the necessary thinking, has explicit hypotheses in mind, and is conducting and controlling the research. This, in itself, will contribute to increased self-esteem.

The list of hypotheses also provides a focus for discussion with family and friends. A couple may be able to sit down together and explore the hypotheses, which provide a structure and therefore make the task easier. This may not only confirm or refute hypotheses already listed, but may lead to alternatives being formulated. In discussing her list of hypotheses with her husband, the mother of the child with asthma found out that she had become very preoccupied and unhappy since the diagnosis, and that this made her husband feel insecure. The possibility that it was her mood that was influencing the difficult behaviour of the child, was given some support. They also derived support for the hypothesis that the father, in contrast to mother, was being too lenient in discipline. He explained this as his needing to make up for his wife's severity, but the effect of their behaviour together, they decided, was inconsistency, which was not good for the child.

Emboldened by her discussions with both the helper and her

husband, this mother went on to do something quite novel for this family – to involve the children directly in discussing her worries. The hypotheses were shared, and her son told her that he thought she did not love him since his asthma began. Although this hurt her, it gave final support to the hypothesis concerning her own role in his difficult behaviour. However, the involvement of the children and the newly found openness in family communication virtually solved the problem.

Observation. Direct observation is a third way of testing, and even suggesting, a whole range of hypotheses. Although we are observing what occurs around us all the time, we rarely have the time to ponder upon the events in a detached frame of mind, or to be systematic in our observations. It can therefore be very helpful for parents to arrange to observe their child, for example, in a more leisurely and useful manner. The example I have chosen illustrates a situation where the concern was with testing the constructions of the meaning of behaviour and not only the causes.

A father, who had become convinced that his son was in constant pain from arthritis, arranged to observe his son unobtrusively. On several occasions, he watched him from the bedroom window while he was playing in the garden with friends. He also discussed his behaviour with his teacher and was able to watch him from a distance in the playground. What he saw was a happy boy, having some trouble getting around, but absorbed and interested in what he was doing and little different from his friends. This, together with discussions with his wife and the teacher, enabled him to see that his son's pain was always more evident when he was with his father. This led him to accept the hypothesis that his son made more of his pain when he was around, and that it was to do with his (the father's) excessive concern.

This father did not necessarily look at specific behaviour. He just tried to see what his son did in various situations, although there was a focus upon pain. There is, however, the possibility of doing more specific observations over longer periods. Parents might count the number of times a child is disobedient over a number of days, or wets his/her pants. One mother made a record of the times her husband was irritable, and discovered that it was almost always on weekends when he was winding down from the demands of his very stressful job. These methods are technically referred to as *event recording*. For events that occur very frequently, an alternative method is to break up the observation period into small time intervals (for example, of five seconds or five minutes) and then to count the number of intervals in which the event happens. To illustrate, a mother recorded the number of five-minute intervals in which her baby was grizzly or cried over a set period of two to three hours each day. This is called *interval recording*. Another method is to try to make a more exact measurement by timing the amount of crying (*duration recording*).

These, and other methods, are all potentially useful in helping people to explore their situations and problems. They may provide information that is not already available to parents, and are a means of testing specific hypotheses systematically. Furthermore, such information can provide baseline data against which to compare changes that may result from any attempt at intervention. A practical guide to such methods can be found, for example, in Carr (1980).

Experiments. Making observations as suggested above is a kind of naturalistic experiment, in which parents do not interfere, but just watch what happens. There is, however, the option of conducting more formally controlled experiments to test the various hypotheses that parents derive. Again the possibilities are endless, and determined entirely by the ingenuity of the parents and helper, but some examples will serve to illustrate.

A mother who thought that her daughter's somewhat overactive behaviour was due to her tendency to smother her food with tomato ketchup, carried out the obvious experiment of removing the ketchup from her diet for a week. She kept a record of the child's behaviour during this period, and noticed an improvement. She then reintroduced the sauce, and found an immediate recurrence of the overactivity.

A second example involved a couple who were having problems with the wife's parents. They visited the couple less frequently, and when they did, were irritable and picked quarrels. The couple listed a number of hypotheses, one of which was that the grandparents had begun to feel resentment at being left out of the care of the child, who was newly diagnosed as having epilepsy. They tested this by trying to involve the grandparents and deliberately finding tasks for them to do with the child. Their view was validated by the fact that there was an increased amount of contact, and they became much less argumentative.

Role-play is one very useful method of helping parents to experiment, and I will illustrate this with reference to the rather depressed father described earlier, whose daughter had renal failure. To explore the possibility that it was his own behaviour that made others critical (and alienated his daughter), he agreed to act out a role in his daily life for one week only. We discussed the role at length before it was adopted. The role was derived from a close examination of the self-characterization sketch that he had written and involved him acting the part of a person who was very interested in the feelings, thoughts and words of other people, including his wife and family. The implications of this for his behaviour were worked out between us, and included listening to people carefully and showing his interest by asking questions and commenting positively. Once he was happy with the role, it was adopted throughout his waking life. At the end of the week, in our next meeting, he commented upon the gradual difference that had occurred in his interactions with his family. He had noticed that they had become more prepared to talk to him, much more interested in him and much less likely to be critical. His wife even praised him on one occasion for his interest in her. What was most important, was that his daughter came to him a number of times and even cuddled him. He explained this in terms of having stopped his persistent monitoring of her fluid intake, and learning to trust her to regulate it herself.

The father was able to test hypotheses about the reasons for his unhappiness, poor self-image and specific difficulties with his daughter. His original hypotheses tended to explain his unhappiness in terms of a natural incompetence relative to other people (for example, 'a born worrier' with poor understanding and poor problem-solving skills). He used his family's rather critical reactions as evidence. In contrast, what he learned from his experiment was that he could control and change his own behaviour, that he was not as incompetent as he had thought, that he could influence the reactions of others, and that they did not necessarily think that he was incompetent. He discovered that it was his own self-preoccupation and inability to trust others that made him appear interfering and critical, therefore alienating others.

This technique is closely related to what Kelly called *fixed role therapy*, which is described in detail in Kelly (1991). It is a very effective way of helping parents to experiment with the hypotheses they have about themselves, their behaviour and their relationship to other people. The focus upon acting is an important aspect of the technique because, while parents may not feel able to change themselves successfully and permanently, they may feel more secure and more capable of change if they feel that it is only pretending, and for a limited period. Asking someone to *act as though* they were happy, may help them change more effectively than, for example, telling them just to pull themselves together and get on with it.

Similar role-play techniques can also be used in actual sessions with the helper – a relatively safe environment in which the parents can be encouraged to set up a variety of scenes and to act them out. This is not only a way of testing hypotheses, but also a way of learning about situations that are otherwise difficult to face. Coping skills and strategies can also be acquired and practised in such sessions.

This is what happened with a woman who was having difficulties with her father-in-law. She described the way he interfered in the treatment of her son who had disabilities arising from a spinal injury, and how he constantly criticized her for spoiling him. The criticism hurt her deeply, but she had not been able to deal with it, partly because of her own guilt over the child's injury and partly because he meant well and, in other ways, was a great support to her. In exploring the problem with her helper, she listed several hypotheses explaining the father-in-law's behaviour. Several of the reasons were easy to refute by discussion, but there came a point where the only way of testing the remaining hypotheses, was to discuss the whole situation with the father-in-law personally. She felt uneasy about doing this, because it meant making her feelings known to him, and she was frightened about how he would react. What she did, therefore, with the helper was to discuss ways of raising the issue with the father-in-law, and then acted out the various suggestions. The helper took the part of the father-in-law and was able to feed back his reactions to the mother, and together they decided upon what they thought were the best strategies. As a result, the actual discussion with the father-in-law turned out to be a lot less stressful than anticipated and led to a successful solution.

Concluding Remarks

I have tried to give an indication in this chapter of the strategies involved in helping parents to change their constructions, so that they develop models that are more useful in facilitating their adaptation to events and in resolving difficulties. We have now covered the most important aspects of providing basic counselling support for parents. We have looked at the processes and skills of developing an appropriate relationship and of helping parents to explore the problems facing them. With the skills of challenging considered in the present chapter, potential helpers have the basic ability to facilitate parental adaptation. With this help, parents will be more able to cope and help themselves effectively. However, there will always be specific problems that parents have to resolve, and this will be the concern of the next chapter. This focuses on the skills necessary to help parents to set goals on the basis of the models they have formulated, to plan and carry out strategies for meeting these goals, and to evaluate the outcomes.

Summary

❑ An integral part of the helping process involves the facilitation of change in the ways parents (or their children) view the events of their world.

❑ The most important and dramatic example of this is the disclosure interview in which parents are given the news of their child's diagnosis.

❑ Detailed attention is given to the breaking of bad news, because it is often done badly, contributing to the distress and dissatisfaction of parents.

❑ Breaking bad news involves careful preparation in terms of deciding who should tell what to whom, when, where and how. The consultation involves all the skills and qualities discussed previously in the book, beginning with discovering what the parents already know, fear or expect.

❑ On this basis, they can be given the relevant information about the diagnosis – directly, clearly and simply.

❑ It is important not to overload parents with information at this stage, but rather to be responsive to their reactions, wishes and questions.

❑ The interview should end with a clear plan for the future (especially an early follow-up appointment) and appropriate consideration for the immediate support needed if parents are still in shock.

❑ Many other changes are likely to be required of parents with children who are chronically ill and the specific skills for facilitating such change are described as challenging skills.

❑ Such challenges should be offered tentatively, within a trusting relationship, and for the explicit benefit of the parents. They should be clear, concise, concrete, specific and positive.

❑ Challenging skills include: giving information, summarizing, self-disclosure, advanced empathy, immediacy and confrontation.

❑ More general strategies involve sharing with parents the notion that the ways we see events are, in fact, hypotheses, and that there always are alternatives.

❑ Each hypothesis must be clearly formulated and then tested for validity and usefulness in resolving a problem.

❑ Testing may occur through discussion with the helper or others, by observation, or by direct experimentation.

6

Problem-solving

In their first meeting with the parent adviser, it became clear that the parents had a desperate, consuming passion to find a cure for their son's disease, although after four years the diagnosis was still uncertain, treatment was only palliative and the child was unlikely to survive much longer. They felt unsupported and ill-informed about the disease and its treatment. Although desperate, they felt passive, unable to do anything and completely in the hands of the professionals, by whom they felt dominated. They felt no control over tests and treatments, most of which seemed futile to them, and guaranteed only to cause pain for their son, who was terrified of all medical staff. They were extremely concerned about the effects of what they saw as the abnormal life to which he was exposed, on his development and personality. The child spent little time at home. As a result, the other children rarely saw their mother and were suffering emotionally and socially, showing behavioural problems. The parents rarely saw each other and had obvious relationship difficulties.

Their overall model was one of general confusion, uncertainty in relation to all areas of their lives, helpless passivity, and an obsession with cure. However, following systematic exploration of their construct systems (including disease and death, the paediatricians, the child, their own role, their other children and what they felt was important in life), they changed dramatically. They became much clearer about all their problems, began to take control and to aim for quality of life for the whole family, and not cure for the child at all costs. They came to ignore the illness as much as possible, to decide what they wanted in terms of treatment, and attempted to normalize the life of both the child and the family. Overall, they became positive, had direction, and were much more able to cope.

The changes in this family, in the ways they construed themselves and their situation, resulted directly from the opportunity to interact with a helper, who enabled them to explore their construct systems. They were much better adapted to their situation as a result. There remained, however, a series of specific problems that they went on to tackle, including behavioural difficulties with the children. Their new understanding formed the basis for this – enabling them to set clear goals, to plan how to achieve them, to implement the plans, and to evaluate the results. It is with the helper skills involved in facilitating this that the present chapter is concerned. For an in-depth analysis of these issues the work of Egan (1982) is recommended.

Goal-setting

Once parents have clarified their constructions, they are in a better position to decide upon appropriate *aims* (that is, the general directions in which they want to go) and *goals* (that is, their specific objectives). In the family above, their aim changed from the search for a cure at all costs to focusing upon the quality of living. Their goals included: having at least 30 minutes a day together as a couple away from the children and the illness; spending at least one afternoon a week with the siblings on an outing chosen by them; spending no more than one day a week at the hospital; and involving themselves in all treatment decisions.

Whatever parents decide as goals, it is important they be formulated appropriately, otherwise their plans will be poorly directed and outcomes will be difficult to evaluate. A mother who had been struggling to stop her nine-year-old from soiling his trousers (the implicit goal) did not notice that she had actually reduced the frequency of the soiling by half, and still regarded herself as failing. It is, therefore, worth thinking about criteria for setting useful goals in order to enable parents to direct their efforts as productively as possible.

Criteria for setting goals

Acceptability. The first criterion of a useful goal is that the primary responsibility for the decision rests with the parents, so that it is in keeping with their values. The helper may have different goals and is free to discuss and negotiate these with parents, but it is very important not to impose them. This can happen very easily given the power of the professional, as in the case of a family who allowed their son's cancer to be treated aggressively, although it was known that there was little hope of recovery. The parents watched their child suffer the ravages of chemotherapy, and then watched him die. They came to feel very sad and enormously guilty for agreeing to the treatment, and were angry with the medical staff because they felt the decision had been imposed on them, without adequate information. Another example of professionals being insensitive to the needs of the family is that of a surgeon who went out of his way to persuade a family to have yet another kidney transplant after a series of failures. The ill daughter had already decided against it and had also decided to stop dialysis with her parents' agreement. They were resigned to their daughter dying with dignity, only to find themselves badgered into changing their minds. They were able to resist these overtures, but experienced enormous rudeness and distress as a result.

Parents should be helped to consider both what they *think* they should do, and what they *want* to do. That is, they should try to explore and be clear about the pressures on them from family, friends, professionals or others, and to be able to distinguish these from their own views. For example, a mother began her session with me by saying that she did not want her son to be told of his imminent death. During our discussion, however, it became clear that it was her husband who was insisting upon silence, whereas she wanted to talk to her child who, so she thought, knew anyway. Rather than living with this failure to communicate for the rest of her life, she addressed the issue directly with her husband, and then decided to act herself and talk openly to the child.

Accomplishments. Each goal should be expressed as an accomplishment or an objective, not as the process by which it is to be reached. 'I would like him to be able to fill the syringe on his own' is the specification of a goal, whereas 'I want to teach him to fill the syringe' is more a description of the process by which a goal is to be achieved.

Clear and specific. Goals should clearly express an end-product that should be as specific as possible. 'To get on better as a couple' is a general aim that may be more clearly stated as a number of specific goals, such as 'Not to quarrel about the treatment', 'Eating at least one leisurely meal together a week when the children have gone to bed', and 'Talking about household matters and making decisions together'. There again, 'Improving the child's behaviour' is a rather general aim, that can more usefully be formulated as 'Reducing the number of times he fights with his brother' or 'Being able to put her to bed without a struggle'.

Observable. Whereas aims are more general and their achievement is not always easy to assess directly, goals should be formulated in ways that allow parents to know clearly whether they have been achieved. Failing to do this accounted for the mother mentioned above feeling she had failed in her efforts to change her child's soiling. 'Teaching my child to read' is an aim expressed as a process, the achievement of which is impossible to determine. 'He should be able to recognize three words by the end of the week' is a goal, the achievement of which can be determined easily.

To be able to assess the achievement of goals in this way usually requires that parents are aware of the point at which they started. A goal such as, 'To reduce the number of tantrums' is only measurable if the parent has a baseline against which to assess the change. Prior exploration of the problems should ensure that parents have such knowledge.

Realistic and adequate. Another criterion for workable goals is that they are realistic. This means that there should be a reasonable expectation of them being achieved. However, they should also be adequate, in the sense of not being set at such a low level as to make little significant difference to the problem identified. Curing Down's syndrome is not possible, but enabling the child to acquire specified developmental skills is realistic, given that the pre-existing developmental level of the child must be taken into account. On the other hand, helping a child to swear only 199 times a day as opposed to 200, contributes almost nothing and is therefore inadequate.

It is important to know where one begins with the problem (for example, the number of arguments or the level of a child's existing skills) in order to gauge the level of change required. One may have to think about both long-term and short-term goals. For example, although the long-term goal may be a child taking complete responsibility for her insulin injection, this may be achieved via a series of short-term goals, such as injecting under supervision, injecting without supervision, loading the syringe under supervision and loading without, and so on.

Factors that affect how realistic or adequate goals are include: the extent to which parents have the necessary resources (for example, the money for a pioneering operation in another country, the skills to improve communication with professionals); obstacles to the achievement of the goal (for example, massive waiting lists); the extent to which the goal is in the parents' control (for example, other children in the class may prevent the child from concentrating and learning); and the cost–benefit balance (for example, the chances of dying on the operating table may outweigh the chances of success, the hours needed to exercise the child may prevent any other family life).

Time-limit. The final criterion is that each goal should incorporate a realistic time-limit. If a mother is to attempt to leave her child at playgroup on his/her own, then she should have some idea of how long it will take to achieve this, in order to be able to evaluate the outcome. If the goal is to gain the child's cooperation with his/her treatment regime, it is important to have some estimate of how long one might expect to take in achieving the goal, since otherwise one would not know when to evaluate the strategy adopted and hence to change it if necessary.

Helping parents set goals

In helping parents to decide goals, all the skills discussed earlier in the book are relevant. The fundamental attitudes (see Chapter 4) and the skills of attending, active listening, prompting, empathy, exploring and challenging are all essential, since the parent–helper relationship is no less important, and exploration of issues continues, albeit at a different stage in the helping process.

It may be obvious what goals are to be set, and only limited discussion is required to formulate them. In other instances, however, the process may be very difficult. For example, following discussion with the surgeon, parents were unable to decide whether to agree to cardiac surgery with a high risk of death on the operating table. Therefore, with the help of their parent adviser, they focused upon their general aims and goals, prior to making the decision. The discussion was painful, involving an exploration of their self-constructions, their role in relation to the child and their religious beliefs. They eventually decided that their goal was to minimize the child's suffering and not to fulfil their own ('selfish') need to have their only child with them for as long as possible. As a consequence, they opted for surgery and, although the child died and they were bereft, they never doubted that their decision was correct.

As always in making decisions, it is useful to begin with a range of the options from which to choose. To facilitate the process of deciding goals when they are not obvious, the parent and helper might work together to list, and write down, all possible options. This may be done by brainstorming (see below) or by a technique of imagining different futures (Egan, 1986). This involves asking parents to try to imagine scenes from a future in which their problem was solved. By discussion, these scenes can then be used to generate a number of useful goals from which to choose.

To illustrate, a woman was asked to imagine future scenes if her husband were to be more supportive in the care of their son, Tim, who had paraplegia. By doing this, she moved from the general aim of 'being more helpful' to specific scenes sampled here:

> *He would get home from work in time to bath Tim.*
> *He would take Tim for trips in the car to give her a break.*
> *He would take responsibility for getting repeat prescriptions.*
> *He would accompany her on Tim's six-monthly clinic checks.*

From these scenes or from other possibilities generated by discussion, clear goals may be formulated and selected. This requires that each be discussed fully, formulated in terms of the criteria described earlier, and decisions made about whether it is to be pursued. A way of doing this is to take each goal in turn and to list both its positive and negative implications. For the scene above, where the woman's husband accompanied her to the clinic, examples of the positive implications were that she would be more able to cope with the journey, less anxious, and more likely to remember what the consultant said. On the negative side, she listed loss of earnings, her husband's work position being threatened, and him having to catch up and therefore arriving home even later in the evening. Such implications can be considered carefully, giving as reasonable a basis as possible for the final selection of goals.

Planning Action

Once their goals have been clearly formulated, parents are in a position to plan how they may best be achieved. This is a step that is often taken in more of a hurry than is necessary, again without considering all the possible options. As always, the parents should be, and feel, fully involved in the discussion, with all options negotiated between the helper and parents. It is crucial for parents' self-esteem and feelings of effectiveness that they not only make final decisions, but they generate for themselves as many ideas as possible.

Setting priorities

If there are a number of goals, the parents first have to establish priorities to decide the order in which they should be tackled. This might mean dealing with just one issue at a time before returning to focus upon the next goal at a future session. On the other hand, more than one goal may need to be considered together, particularly if they are closely related. It is important to be careful that too much is not attempted so that parents become overburdened.

Brainstorming

Having determined priorities, the parents are invited to focus upon one goal at a time, and to take the lead in thinking up possible strategies for action. The technique of brainstorming is useful here, since it is essentially an exercise concerned with encouraging creativity or divergent thinking. As in deciding goals, the idea here is to help the parents make explicit every conceivable strategy so as to be in a position to select the best single option or combination.

This can be done with pencil and paper or a flip-chart on which are written all the strategies produced by the exercise. The parents are asked to go on producing as many ideas as they can until they have exhausted their creativity. They should be encouraged to let themselves go and not to evaluate any of the ideas at this stage. They should just list them all, no matter how good, bad or far-fetched they seem to be at the time; evaluation comes later. If at all possible, it should be a pleasurable activity, in which the parents exercise their problem-solving skills and enjoy both the power of their thinking and even the silliness of some of the outcomes. It should not, however, go on so long as to become boring and tedious.

The helper should engage in the activity with the parents by encouraging them to continue, praising their efforts, possibly adding to the list, but preferably by guiding them so that they grasp ideas for themselves, as opposed to telling them directly. This may involve helping them to clarify (without criticism) the ideas they have, as well as stimulating them to derive further ideas from, for example, combinations of the ones they have listed. The parents may be prompted by asking what they have tried in the past; what other people have suggested or tried; who they might approach for advice/help; whether they know other people who are coping with similar problems; whether there are relevant organizations that may be useful; and whether there are ready-made programmes that might be of value (for example, home teaching projects). Whatever the helper does, it should be supportive and encouraging. To illustrate the process, a mother whose son had a bad facial disfigurement, sought help with his anxieties about school. After extensive discussion, a clear model of the problem was formed, and two interrelated goals were formulated: firstly, to increase the boy's ability to deal with his peers and, secondly, to stop their taunting and bullying. A few of the mother's suggestions derived from brainstorming were:

➤ *Punish every child who hurts him.*
➤ *Teach the child to fight and hit the bullies.*

➤ *Teach him to ignore them.*
➤ *Teach him how to engage and get on with his peers.*
➤ *Find the bullies and talk to their parents.*
➤ *Get angry with the teachers.*
➤ *Change his school.*
➤ *Keep him at home all the time.*
➤ *Complain to the governors.*
➤ *Talk to the education authorities.*
➤ *Look at the research on bullying.*
➤ *Contact a voluntary organization concerned with disfigurement.*
➤ *Talk calmly to the class teacher expressing her anxieties.*
➤ *Talk to the head.*
➤ *Show a video at school on disfigurement.*
➤ *Find a friend/protector for her son at school.*

Choosing strategies

Having produced as many options as possible, the next step is to go through the list and evaluate each of them very carefully, because even strategies that seem ridiculous or impossible may contain the seeds of a brilliant idea. Each item should be considered separately. This can be tackled by discussion, gradually eliminating options to leave only the most useful. However, there are various ways of making the discussion systematic, by, for example, doing a cost–benefit analysis. This involves: 1) deciding how beneficial the given strategy is likely to be in meeting the formulated goals; 2) deciding what the costs, in the widest sense, would be; and 3) deciding whether the necessary resources are available.

For instance, the mother in the example just given thought that teaching her child to fight might have some benefit, because 'other children would stop bullying and would think twice about teasing him'. However, the costs were high, in that her son might get hurt; he would probably get into trouble with the teachers; it would not have the positive effect of making him liked by others; and aggression was against the mother's values. In terms of resources, this option was further limited by the fact that he was very small, poorly coordinated in comparison with his peers, and extremely anxious by nature, as opposed to aggressive. This option was therefore deleted.

On the other hand, going to see the class teacher to express her anxieties was eventually accepted as the top of the list of options. The mother thought that it would be beneficial in that it would be the means by which other strategies would be implemented. She felt the teacher would shed light on the situation, would be concerned, would be motivated by parental support, and would have valuable methods to suggest. There were costs, however, in that it went against the mother's principles of not being an interfering parent, and it involved her own anxieties of approaching figures of authority. She had the resources in terms of time, but she lacked the social skills to approach the teacher calmly, without appearing threatening or passive.

Having gone through the list and removed unacceptable and ineffective options, and possibly modified others, the remainder can be compared in order to make final decisions. The selection process may be helped by having in mind the same criteria described in choosing goals. Plans finally chosen will be most effective if they are acceptable to the parents; clear and specific; realistic and adequate; set within appropriate time-limits and if they have observable effects in relation to the goal. It may also be possible to place them in an order of preference. However, when there are several equally good options, then decisions are required about implementing them sequentially or simultaneously.

The aim overall is to select the most effective strategies for achieving the decided goals. Although there is never a guarantee of absolute success, the more careful the selection from all possible options, and the more thought given to the skills needed to carry out the course of action and the likely difficulties to be encountered, the greater the likelihood of success.

Implementing Plans

Before an attempt is made to implement the plans, it is important to give careful consideration to difficulties that might occur. If they are forewarned about possible obstacles, parents will be in a better position to deal with them. For example, parents who were planning to try to ignore their child's excessive tantrum behaviour will benefit from realizing that the behaviour may well get worse prior to improving. This kind of exploration will enable them to prepare in the most effective way, and to have contingency plans ready if necessary.

It is also important to prepare carefully in terms of the resources that may be required (for example, the telephone number or address of an organization, the money to travel to a remote centre, the time, energy and equipment to carry out a programme of exercises). The parents may need to acquire a variety of skills. In the case of the mother going to talk to the teacher, it was decided that she should not arrive unannounced either before or after the school day, because the teacher would be unprepared and may not have adequate time for her. She therefore decided to leave a note asking for an appointment. She also anticipated having difficulties in communicating as she was extremely shy and was concerned about saying clearly what she meant. She therefore role-played the scene several times with the helper (who acted as the teacher) so that she felt more prepared and confident.

Strategies may vary from the parents going to the library to find information, to consulting another professional, such as a social worker, physiotherapist or physician. A plan of management to deal with emotional or learning difficulties in the child may be instituted, or parents might refer themselves to a marriage counsellor.

Having aided the parents' decision-making and preparation, the role of the helper is to support them while the plans are put into operation. This means being available, valuing and respecting them, which is, in effect, no different from the role advocated throughout the book at all stages. People need encouragement, and all the skills described previously can still be employed to make parents feel good about themselves and believe that they can succeed. This includes lifting them when dispirited, praising their efforts and successes, and helping them deal with unexpected difficulties. You may need to loop back to previous stages, such as exploration or planning.

Evaluation of Care

The next step is evaluation, where the helper and parents consider the outcome of the strategies adopted. It is arbitrary to consider this a separate stage, because it is occurring all the time. However, there should be specific times at which the helper and parents take stock, both of the effects of their plans and their relationship together. Although it is important, it may not be given the time it deserves within the general health care system. Professionals often give advice or prescribe without follow-up, especially in primary care, for example.

After implementing specific plans, the question to be addressed relates to the degree to which the goals have been achieved, and the reasons for the outcomes. If completely successful, then the partnership will move on: to the next goal in a series; to the exploration of a new problem; or to a re-evaluation of the relationship (see next section). Whatever the case, one should try to evaluate what the parents have discovered in their success.

This might include evaluating why the strategy was successful, what factors were important and what the outcome tells parents about the problem. For example, a mother of a child with diabetes had been extremely successful in getting her son to adhere to his diet by calm discussion of the problem with him and negotiated rewards for compliance. In the evaluation, it emerged that she had learnt that, although her original model was that his non-compliance was due to resentment and rebellion, he became compliant when he was allowed to control the situation. The rewards were in his control, but he had also been allowed to discuss the situation with his parents, as opposed to them – especially his father – imposing the diet. The mother also learned that the relationships within the family as a whole had improved, because more open discussion was occurring generally.

The evaluation in this case also involved consideration of the role of the helper, in that the mother began by attributing the success to the advice of the helper. Although highly flattered by this, the helper made her see the reality of the situation, in that it was her own inventiveness and clear thinking and her communication with her son that had been the reasons for the success. She was helped, and this is vital, to own her success, and to see the role of the helper as a catalyst.

Other strategies may not be quite so successful in achieving the desired goals and evaluation is particularly important in discovering the reasons for this. The planned strategies may not have been carried out, perhaps because other problems arose and prevented the implementation of the plans. On the other hand, they may have been carried out inappropriately, or they may just have failed. For example, a mother had been unable to express her dissatisfaction to her paediatrician as she had planned, because he had been charming in contrast to his usual rudeness. A couple failed to implement a strategy of rewards to try to increase their daughter's compliance with her diet for diabetes, because they were unable to negotiate specific rewards with her. A mother failed to decrease her child's night-time crying, because she could not bear to leave him to cry for the time it would have taken. One woman had spent time with her husband each day as planned, but had hated it. Another couple had listened to their own parents carefully and used all the skills possible to resolve a difficulty with them, but they had still been critical and dogmatic.

Each case has to be explored carefully and new strategies planned. This may mean simply implementing the same plan in a modified form, or helping parents overcome the difficulty experienced, or it may involve going back to earlier stages of the helping process. For example, the goals set may have been inappropriate or unrealistic, or the model used to formulate the goals in the first place may have been inaccurate. By attempting the strategy, however, it could work as a kind of experiment through which valuable feedback is made available, leading one to recommence the helping process at the exploration stage so that a more adequate model can be built and more appropriate goals devised. It might be that parents misjudged their child's existing skills in administering his/her own insulin and therefore had to set more limited goals before the child could take over the responsibility. In another example, a couple had stopped their son wetting his bed as planned, but instead he wet his bedroom floor. In evaluating this, they came to see that their original model of inadequate training was incorrect, and that it was his fear of the trip to the bathroom that was the reason for the problem.

Evaluating the parent–helper relationship

Just as it is important to evaluate outcomes with the parents, so must one periodically assess the parent–helper relationship. This is also true when plans have been implemented successfully, because the question of whether the parents and helper should continue to meet may arise at this point. There is, however, the need to monitor continually whether the relationship is adequate, whether it could be more productive, or even if it has become destructive, for example, in encouraging dependency in the parents. It is important, therefore, that from the beginning there are opportunities for the parents to negotiate honestly with the helper whether and how their relationship should continue.

Such discussion is not easy, because there may be a strong tendency for the parents not to be totally open about their feelings, so as not to hurt the helper. Parents protect professionals constantly. There is, however, also the danger of the helper inadvertently giving the impression that he/she does not want to continue with the relationship.

There are no simple and specific answers to these difficulties. To a large extent, they depend upon the nature of the relationship developed between the parents and helper. If it is mutually respectful, trusting and honest, with the parents' needs as central, then a truthful discussion is more likely. More specifically, the skills of *immediacy* are vital here (see Chapter 5). Acknowledging explicitly the difficulty with such discussion, but the need for absolute honesty, may also be useful.

Although there should be support available to parents at all times, there are times at which it is appropriate for the parents and helper to stop meeting, or to reduce the frequency with which they do so. This may be at the request of the parents or the helper, but the final decision should be negotiated. If the parents do not want to continue, even if the helper disagrees, their decision should be respected, although an attempt to negotiate is appropriate. If the helper is leaving the district and must stop seeing the family, or thinks that the family are strong enough to continue on their own with only occasional visits, then again this must be negotiated.

It is important, however, that plenty of warning be given of such change. There should be time for the parents to adapt and to consider the implications with the helper beforehand. The helper should not withhold the information until the last minute under the misapprehension that this will avoid hurting them. Allowing some months and several meetings of warning gives the opportunity not only to explore how the parents will manage in the future without the helper, but will usually prevent the pain of separation from being exaggerated by misunderstandings. It is not unusual for parents to be hurt and resentful at the prospect of losing a beneficial relationship, and they should be allowed to express and explore this. There is no way to prevent the hurt, since all effective helpers will be missed, but the process of leaving may be used as a learning opportunity, and not as an addition to the difficulties parents have already.

Dependency is always an issue with which one has to struggle in the business of helping. Again there are no easy answers, but if one is concerned throughout one's contact with parents to foster their self-esteem and self-efficacy, the potential destructiveness of dependency can be avoided. As noted earlier, the role of the helper is to highlight the parents' own role and effectiveness in coping with chronic disease and its consequences, and not to emphasize the skills of the helper.

Useful Strategies

I have deliberately avoided describing specific strategies for helping with the various problems facing parents. This is largely because I have wanted to stress the importance of relating to parents appropriately and providing general support that enables their own resources to be mobilized along with their own creative adaptation and problem-solving. I have also done this, because strategies to be adopted have to be tailored to suit the unique problem of the family. Although a cookbook approach may provide the feeling of competence and confidence for the helper, ready available off-the-peg strategies provided by the helper may not be the best way of fostering the competence and confidence of the family. Even if I feel, with a specific family, that I know a technique that will help resolve a particular problem, I do all that I can to help them derive the idea for themselves, as opposed to telling them what they should do.

There are, however, many strategies of possible value to parents in facing all the kinds of problems and issues described in Chapter 2. These derive from the vast range of literature relating to psychology generally, and to the areas of health psychology, counselling and psychotherapy in particular. It is always wise to read as widely as possible, and to discover the kinds of strategies and other resources (both local and national) that are available to you in your work with parents. To help you begin this process, I should like to suggest a few directions to explore, as well as some useful references.

Relating to children

The focus of the book has deliberately been upon parents as explained earlier. The assumption has been made that, in general, the helper will relate first and foremost to the parents, to enable them to help their child themselves. However, there are times when the professional will have to communicate with children directly. For example, professionals have direct responsibility for children in hospital, or children may want to address problems with the professional. There are also occasions when parents may ask the professional to counsel their child.

Knowing how to communicate directly with children is, therefore, essential. However, helpers need to have such knowledge also to enable parents themselves to communicate more effectively with their child. The helper is frequently concerned with problems in the parent–child relationship and should be in a position to help the parents deal with these effectively. If he/she has a good understanding of the basic skills of counselling, then these can be shared with parents for the benefit of their understanding of and relationship with their child.

Although communicating with children merits a text on its own, it must be said that the basic principles and skills of such communication are the same as those that have been described in this book. This is true even though children may function differently from adults intellectually, and may communicate in different ways. The processes of establishing a mutually trusting relationship, providing the opportunity for the child to talk, exploring the situation thoroughly from the child's viewpoint, negotiating aims, and so on are as important in professional–child or parent–child communication as they are in professional–parent communication. The qualities of respect, humility, genuineness, empathy and quiet enthusiasm are equally important here. The skills of attending, prompting, active listening and the others described in the book are crucial, although the vehicle may be different, and it may not be quite so easy.

The vehicle of communication may be direct conversation, depending upon factors such as the child's age, ability and temperament. However, it may be that one has to use play as a means of communicating; using toys, water, sand, books, pictures, drawing or whatever else will engage the child. Difficulties arise from the fact that the child may have such a different construct system from the adult that it may not be easy to grasp the models that the child is using to anticipate the events in her/his world. Nevertheless, if one really accepts that all communication begins with a grasp of the other's viewpoint, and one must listen very carefully to do so, such differences will emerge.

A useful book about communicating with children and general parenting skills is by Sokolov and Hutton (1988). Valuable texts on helping parents to teach children skills in the context of general developmental delay are by Carr (1980) and Cunningham and Sloper (1978). These include information on dealing with behavioural and emotional problems, but an excellent book on this specifically is by Herbert (1988). Useful ideas can also be found in Hoghughi (1988).

Of particular importance is the area of preparing children for admission to hospital; for painful and invasive procedures, such as lumbar punctures, taking blood, wound debridement in burns, and for surgery. There is also the very sad, but necessary, task of talking to children about death, including their own and that of others close to them. Eiser (1990), Whitehead (1989), and Pruitt and Elliott (1990) provide valuable information and directions for dealing with these issues.

What is perhaps most important in dealing with these areas is honesty, giving necessary information to the child in ways she/he can understand, and not misguidedly trying to protect children by concealment. Wherever possible, children should be helped to prepare themselves by having information in advance, having the opportunity to discuss what is to occur, and having permission to show their feelings openly. Events should be as predictable as possible for them, and they should be given as much control over what happens as possible. This may include providing models of procedures in the form of books, pictures, or film material. The opportunity to explore a syringe, for example, or to see it being used, may decrease the anxiety involved for the child. The child may also benefit from learning strategies to control and deal with pain, including relaxation, breathing control, distraction, positive self-talk and imagery. The appropriate use of immediate rewards for self-control, involvement in and control of procedures, and parental coaching have all been used to good effect.

Dealing with related problems

Where parents have difficulties communicating with other people, the helper can enable them to acquire various social skills, and some useful introductory information is available in Nelson-Jones (1988). Again it is pertinent for the helper to share with parents the frameworks and skills that they are themselves using to communicate with the parents. The processes, qualities and skills that have been covered in this book are relevant to communication in all areas, and may be valuable to parents. The skills of assertiveness may be particularly relevant to parents if experiencing difficulties in dealing with professionals, and a very readable book on this topic for both the helper and parents is by Dickson (1982).

Information for helpers interested in the more specialized areas of marital and sexual counselling, which are always useful in family work, is available in Dryden (1985). Treacher and Carpenter (1984) and Barker (1986) are very helpful sources of information about family therapy more generally. Useful and readable books on helping people cope with crises and stress are by Parry (1990) and Fontana (1989). These include practical information on relaxation training, anxiety and stress management, and dealing with depression. More information on cognitive therapy, which is highly relevant here, can be found in Trower, Casey and Dryden (1988). Help with bereavement counselling can be found in Parkes (1978) and Worden (1983).

Concluding Remarks

In this chapter, we have looked at the issue of helping parents to manage specific problems. This includes the steps of, and skills involved in, specifying goals, planning strategies to reach these goals, implementing these plans, and evaluating the results. These steps build upon, and are used in conjunction with, the skills already covered earlier in the book, since these later stages of the helping process can only be implemented once a good relationship has been established with the parents, a thorough exploration of their problems has been conducted, and as clear a model as possible of the problem situations derived.

A detailed consideration of specific techniques and methods that might be of value in working with families of children who are ill and disabled, is beyond the scope of this book. The main concern has been with the development of the basic skills, relevant to all who work with families, of relating to parents, providing negotiated support, and empowering them to adapt to and solve problems themselves. Nevertheless, there is a wide literature on approaches and strategies that is of value to all helpers in the paediatric context.

Some of the approaches, such as marital counselling and family therapy, involve knowledge and skills derived from specialized training. Although the helper can, if motivated, have access to such training, it is more likely for parents to be referred to the appropriate specialist if necessary. The question of referral will be taken up in the final chapter, which will also include consideration of issues of helper training and supervision, evaluation, and the place of psychosocial help in the more general health care system.

Summary

❑ Although helping parents develop clear models for understanding the difficulties confronting them may be all that is required by way of support, there is often a range of specific problems to which they need solutions.

❑ Clear models of the problems provide the basis of the next step in the helping process, that of setting goals.

❑ To be effective, goals should be acceptable to parents, framed in terms of accomplishments, clear and specific, observable, realistic and adequate, and time-limited.

❑ Goals can be formulated through discussion and negotiation, but brainstorming and imagined futures are also useful devices.

❑ The next step in problem management is to plan intervention strategies in partnership with parents. Brainstorming and cost–benefit analysis are valuable techniques to use here.

❑ Implementation involves careful preparation to foresee what resources are required, including the knowledge and skills needed by parents, and the likely problems to be confronted.

❑ The support and encouragement of the helper is of great benefit to parents throughout the implementation stage.

❑ Evaluation is the final step in the process, and includes decisions about the success of the intervention and the reasons for the outcome; improved understanding of the problem; decisions about how to proceed.

❑ Evaluation of the parent–helper relationship is an important part of this process.

❑ The principles and skills described in the book are as relevant to professional–child communication as to professional–parent communication, and can be shared with parents directly in order to facilitate their communication with their children.

❑ Extensive information is available to helpers. Suggested reading is given about parenting skills generally, behavioural, developmental and emotional problems in children, preparation for painful investigative treatment procedures, assertiveness, anxiety and stress management and bereavement counselling.

7

Final Issues

By this point, I hope I have given an indication of the importance of psychosocial care, and that I have provided detailed practical guidance in relation to the processes, skills and qualities involved. Before finishing, there are a number of broader issues that I should like to mention briefly, because it is not sufficient to think of intervention of any kind without some consideration of its broader context, the system within which the ideas described here can operate. Before doing this, however, I should just like to say a little about training.

Training

Although being told what to do is a vital component of skills acquisition, it is impossible to use complex skills proficiently without practice. The skills described here are no exception. To be able to use them to best effect requires the opportunity to use them in a secure context under supervision. This enables the provision of what is arguably the most important element of learning and that is *feedback*. This involves the opportunity to explore what the learner has done, to evaluate it and to see how it can be improved. The skill can then be tried again and again, with further feedback each time, until proficiency is acquired.

Simply applying the skills and strategies described in this book will be beneficial, I have no doubt, but supervised practice with appropriate feedback will not only speed the learning process, but will increase the level of proficiency eventually reached. For maximum benefit, therefore, the reader is advised to seek practice opportunities, and there are a number of possible ways of doing this.

What is required is a small group of people who meet regularly, perhaps once a week for, say, three hours over a period of at least three months, with the intention of training. The meetings might involve discussion and watching videotapes of skilled counselling. Reading between sessions may be a component, as well as supervised work with families. A major component of the sessions, however, is that the participants should take turns in practising the skills on each other. For example, the group can break up into subgroups of three people. One can then act as helper, another as client, while the third person observes. The person being helped should preferably present a personal problem that they are happy to divulge, or alternatively play the role of someone else (for example, a parent) with a problem. At the end of the allotted time (perhaps initially only ten minutes), the people in the group discuss the performance, and provide feedback to the person who acted as the helper. This should always be constructive and positive, starting with the strengths of the participant. Such exercises can be quite stressful until the group develops a high level of trust, and negative feedback can be hurtful and counterproductive. It is preferable to indicate how people should change, than to tell them they have acted poorly. After the discussion, a second member of the group takes a turn at being the helper, and the process is repeated.

Feedback can be given in a number of ways. As indicated above, it can be provided by the group members. Ideally, it might involve someone skilled in the area of communication and counselling acting as a facilitator for the sessions. If the equipment is available, it can also involve recording the practice on videotape, and then discussing the playback. Facilitators for this kind of work may be found in local departments of clinical psychology or in voluntary organizations, educational establishments or in the health services, particularly in primary care.

This kind of practice can be extended further by using actors to simulate parents of children with chronic illnesses. The actors can join in the feedback process with the rest of the group. One may eventually use recordings of real sessions with parents for discussion and feedback. However, this should only be done with the full knowledge and permission of the parents.

For anyone wishing to set up this kind of training, a number of potential resources are available. Such training is slowly becoming a standard part of the undergraduate and postgraduate training for health service personnel, and staff in training schools are acquiring expertise in this field. For example, there are communication skills trainers being employed as lecturers in many of the more forward-looking medical and nursing schools. I have myself run such courses for professionals from the health, education and social services for some years at all levels of the curriculum. Although one might think that this involves a major time commitment, research has shown that a course lasting in the region of 30 to 60 hours spread over a period of about 10 to 12 weeks, can be very effective in improving the ability of professionals to communicate with parents (Rushton and Davis, 1992).

Although courses specializing in work with parents are rare, an alternative is to find and join courses in basic counselling skills that are now being run nationwide by colleges of further education, polytechnics and universities. The British Association for Counselling (BAC) has a directory containing extensive information on these (Chaytor and Palmer, 1992). Similar organizations are available in most other countries. There are also organizations specializing in counselling training who will arrange courses on demand, tailored to the needs of their customers.

Supervision

Learning does not stop after basic training. One must continue to learn by discussion, course attendance and reading. In fact, something can be learnt from every contact with a family, and this is facilitated by having ongoing supervision with someone with expertise in counselling/communication. Ideally, this should be available to all those working in the helping professions to ensure:

- the maintenance of skills;
- the continued enhancement of knowledge and professional abilities;
- the opportunity to look at particular difficulties that arise in practice;
- personal support to avoid the strong possibility of becoming over-burdened and disillusioned when in the situation of facing major human suffering day after day.

Supervision is particularly important in helping people to cope with hearing constant and awful problems from families. However, building upon the models of helping presented here, one should not forget that: you do not have to cure to be helpful; you are not a failure if you do not completely solve all problems; listening and providing respect and dignity to people is valuable in its own right; and being with people in their suffering is a source of such respect.

Although good supervision may not be readily available to most professionals, it is important, particularly when dealing explicitly with the ubiquitous psychological and social problems that are an ever-present and neglected aspect of disease. An attempt may be made to provide supervision as part of the managerial responsibility of direct line managers, but it is not an easy task to combine the roles of manager and supportive supervisor.

System Issues

The question of supervision brings up the whole issue of how the kinds of help I have described fit into the overall system of paediatric health care. Since there is no doubt that there are resource implications (that is, personnel time) of what I am advocating, it has to be admitted that there are no simple solutions at the moment. Current resources are stretched and the situation is worsening, because of increasing demand for physical treatment that becomes increasingly sophisticated, and therefore expensive.

The problem is, however, that the technological emphasis upon the physical has occurred at the expense of the psychological and social, such that neither government not local health care policies give the necessary emphasis to these concerns. In effect, this means inadequate professional training in the skills relating to psychosocial care and a dearth of appropriate resources. There are few, if any people, specifically employed to provide psychosocial care for the family as a whole. What resources are available are used reactively, not preventively, and may be targeted at highly specific problems such as child abuse. The failure of the health services to address psychosocial problems is documented elsewhere (Davis and Fallowfield, 1991). Many professionals do try to take account of broader family issues, but this depends upon the compassion, motivation, and ability of the individual. What is sure, however, is that such help will not be systematically given to all those in need, will not be preventive in orientation, and will not be given by people trained in the skills covered in this book.

My contention is that this could be remedied, not by the full-scale employment of hundreds of specialists, but by the training of all paediatric personnel, and the creation of a system to make maximum use of their skills. This might require an injection of resources in the short-term, but would be more than compensated by the humanistic benefits, and by savings in other areas. For example, if all families were appropriately supported in a proactive way, there would be fewer psychological and social difficulties, parents would be more able to cope independently, and there would be less demand upon frontline services such as general practice, and a reduced need for hospital admission.

I have described such a system (the Parent Adviser Service) elsewhere (Buchan, Clemerson and Davis, 1988) in connection with childhood disability, but this is equally applicable to any chronic disease. The requirements are: 1) close cooperation of all professions working locally; 2) an agreed policy on the need for family-based support; 3) training for all relevant personnel in basic counselling skills; 4) agreement that all personnel will take responsibility for providing general support for a small number of families on an ongoing basis; 5) a system whereby such families are allocated to specific professionals for this care and monitored; and 6) a core team to support, supervise and advise all the people providing direct support. The profession of the specific supporters is irrelevant, provided they are competent at relating well to the family and empowering them by the partnership that they establish. Further personnel may be gained by training volunteers – using parents themselves or by working with the various voluntary organizations involved in this area. The major difficulties here are not resources, but administrative and professional boundaries and competition.

Referral

As in all service work, the person helping families in the way indicated in this book should be clear about their role and expertise. Helpers should never assume knowledge or competence that they do not have, and should, with the humility discussed earlier, be always ready to express ignorance. To do otherwise is of no value whatsoever to families. The possibility of assuming a role for which one is not qualified is unlikely, given the whole ethos of what I have been describing. There is nothing prescriptive in this approach. The skills I have described are those of relating to the family in ways that help them explore, derive clear models, and decide for themselves the most effective strategies for dealing with problems, including seeking appropriate expertise elsewhere.

An assumption in the system to which I alluded in the last section is that all the different professionals should work together more closely, negotiating common aims. An important implication of this is that there is a pool of technical information from these professions readily available to the helper, and hence to the parents. The helper can liaise effectively between the parents and other professionals if necessary. There is also the possibility of joint consultations, which can be enormously beneficial for parents, who might derive security from their helper and therefore use the consultation with another professional more profitably.

Close teamwork also makes referral for specialist help easier. Although there should be no hesitation in referring a family (with their agreement), there is no reason why the helper should not discuss and explore any issues with them, even those directly relevant to another profession. If this helps the parents to think clearly about a problem, it can be to their advantage. It might, for example, enable them to make a clear list of symptoms for when they see the paediatrician, or to know what questions they need to ask. This may mean that they will be able to make the most effective and economical use of the referral. For example, a helper not trained in marital counselling may decide in conjunction with parents that a referral is appropriate. This does not, however, preclude the helper from exploring the relationship difficulties with the parents, enabling them to develop a clearer picture of the problems, and helping them to decide to whom they should be referred. There is also no reason why the helper should not continue to be in touch with the family when they are seeing the specialist.

Evaluation

The final issue to consider is the question of the effectiveness of the ideas we have been discussing. Is there any point in changing the way we practise and developing better communication skills if there is no benefit to the families concerned?

The first answer to this question is based on principle. There is a need for intervention directed at the psychosocial problems confronting families in the context of chronic disease, and there is no other way of providing this except by relating closely to the family and communicating effectively with them. The ideal is, of course, to cure the illness or disability with appropriate organic medicine, and therefore to remove the source of the psychosocial stress and distress. However, there are no such cures for the disorders we have been considering, so psychosocial help is all that is available.

The second answer is empirical and involves searching for evidence of effectiveness, and this comes from several sources. The first is the research on general counselling and psychotherapy. Although there remain many unanswered questions about the processes by which counselling works, the evidence is that there are indeed positive benefits overall. An extensive review of this area is provided by Lambert, Shapiro and Bergin (1986).

The second source of evidence relates to general health care, and has been reviewed by Davis and Fallowfield (1991a). They found considerable support for a number of hypotheses that related the provision of good counselling and communication to: 1) increased professional satisfaction and decreased stress; 2) improved diagnostic accuracy; 3) increased patient satisfaction; 4) improved treatment adherence; 5) positive psychological consequences for patients with a variety of diseases; 6) improved understanding, greater retention of information and better skills; 7) positive benefits in relation to the physical outcomes of the disease; and 8) prevention.

The final evidence, limited only by the dearth of research in the area, concerns studies conducted specifically within the area of paediatrics. Pless and Satterwhite (1972) looked at non-professional counsellors who worked with mothers of children with chronic illnesses and found evidence suggestive of improved psychological adaptation in the children. Stein and Jessop (1984) found evidence of significantly improved child adjustment and maternal satisfaction as the result of a home care support programme, with later evidence that the benefits were sustained (Pless and Nolan, 1991). Finally, and more recently, Davis and Rushton (1991) evaluated the Parent Adviser Scheme, where home visitors were trained in the use of the skills and frameworks described in this book and worked with families of children with severe intellectual and multiple disabilities. In comparison with randomly allocated controls, the mothers who worked with a parent adviser were significantly improved in psychosocial adaptation at the end of the study, and their children had fewer behaviour problems and made significantly better developmental progress.

The overall conclusion, therefore, is that families are likely to benefit by the provision of skilled psychosocial intervention alongside the organic treatment of their difficulties.

Final Words

For me, there is no doubt that families of children with chronic illnesses and disabilities should have routine provision of broad based psychosocial care. At least, they should be given the option of such care throughout their contact with services. I stress this, because there remains considerable parental dissatisfaction with the ways in which professionals relate to parents, and there is much distress that is never seen.

I sincerely hope that this book contributes to the resolution of these problems. My intention has been to make the reader feel more confident and competent in listening to parents and their children respectfully, in working with them in partnership, in enhancing their dignity, and in making them feel good about themselves as people, regardless of the physical and social problems they face.

Whether I have succeeded is for each reader to judge. There are skills to learn and processes to understand better, but there are no absolute rules for helping. Each helper is different; each parent is unique. The interactions between them are rarely routinely predictable. Nevertheless, I hope that each helper will quickly come to realize the enormous influence they can have as a person, and strive to harness the power of their own personality for the benefit of the families they serve. Such power can equal or exceed the breadth and depth of benefits derived from focusing upon physical treatment alone.

References

Bannister, D. and Fransella, F. (1986) *Inquiring Man*. London: Croom Helm.

Barker, P. (1986) *Basic Family Therapy*. London: Collins.

Buchan, L., Clemerson, J. and Davis, H. (1988) Working with families of children with special needs: The Parent Adviser Scheme. *Child: Care, Health and Development, 14*, 81–91.

Byard, O. (1991) David. In A. Cooper and V. Harpin (Eds) *This is Our Child: How Parents Experience the Medical World*. Oxford: Oxford University Press.

Cadman, D., Boyle, M., Szatmari, P. and Offord, D. (1987) Chronic illness, disability, and mental and social well-being: Findings of the Ontario Child Health Study. *Pediatrics, 79*, 805–813.

Carr, J. (1980) *Helping Your Handicapped Child*. Harmondsworth: Penguin.

Chaytor, D. and Palmer, I. (1992) *Training in Counselling and Psychotherapy: A Directory*. Rugby: BAC. Contact BAC, 1 Regent Place, Rugby CV21 2PJ (0788 578328).

Cooper, A. and Harpin, V. (Eds) (1991) *This is Our Child: How Parents Experience the Medical World*. Oxford: Oxford University Press.

Cunningham, C., Morgan, P. and McGucken, R. (1984) Down's syndrome: Is dissatisfaction with disclosure of diagnosis inevitable? *Developmental Medicine and Child Neurology, 26*, 33–39.

Cunningham, C. and Sloper, P. (1978) *Helping Your Handicapped Baby*. London: Souvenir Press.

Davis, H. and Fallowfield, L. (1991a) Evaluating the effects of counselling and communication. In H. Davis and L. Fallowfield (Eds) *Counselling and Communication in Health Care*. Chichester: Wiley.

Davis, H. and Fallowfield, L. (1991b) Counselling and communication in health care: the current situation. In H. Davis and L. Fallowfield (Eds) *Counselling and Communication in Health Care*. Chichester: Wiley.

Davis, H. and Fallowfield, L. (1991c) Counselling theory. In H. Davis and L. Fallowfield (Eds) *Counselling and Communication in Health Care*. Chichester: Wiley.

Davis, H. and Rushton, R. (1991) Counselling and supporting parents of children with developmental delay: a research evaluation. *Journal of Mental Deficiency Research, 35*, 89–113.

Davis, H., Stroud, A. and Green, L. (1989) Child characterization sketch. *International Journal of Personal Construct Psychology, 2*, 323–337.

Dickson, A. (1982) *A Woman in Your Own Right*. London: Quartet.

Dryden, W. (1985) *Marital Therapy in Britain*. London: Harper and Row.

Dryden, W. (1990) *Rational-Emotive Counselling in Action*. London: Sage.

Egan, G. (1982) *The Skilled Helper*, 2nd ed. Monterey: Brooks/Cole.

Egan, G. (1986) *The Skilled Helper*, 3rd ed. Monterey: Brooks/Cole.

Eiser, C. (1990) *Chronic Childhood Disease*. Cambridge: Cambridge University Press.

Fontana, D. (1989) *Managing Stress*. Leicester: British Psychological Society/ Routledge.

Fransella, F. and Dalton, P. (1990) *Personal Construct Counselling in Action.* London: Sage.

Garrison, W. and McQuiston, S. (1989) *Chronic Illness During Childhood and Adolescence.* Newbury Park: Sage.

Herbert, M. (1988) *Working with Children and Their Families.* Leicester: British Psychological Society/Routledge.

Hogbin, B. and Fallowfield, L. (1989) Getting it taped: the bad news consultation with cancer patients. *British Journal of Hospital Medicine, 41,* 330–333.

Hoghughi, M. (1988) *Treating Problem Children: Issues, Methods, and Practice.* London: Sage.

Hughes, P. and Lieberman, S. (1990) Troubled parents: Vulnerability and stress in childhood cancer. *British Journal of Medical Psychology, 63,* 53–64.

Kelly, G. (1991) *The Psychology of Personal Constructs.* London: Routledge.

Lambert, M., Shapiro, D. and Bergin, A. (1986) The effectiveness of psychotherapy. In S. Garfield and A. Bergin (Eds) *Handbook of Psychotherapy and Behaviour Change.* New York: Wiley.

Nelson-Jones, R. (1988) *Practical Counselling and Helping Skills.* London: Cassell.

Parkes, C. (1978) *Bereavement: Studies of Grief in Adult Life.* Harmondsworth: Penguin.

Parry, G. (1990) *Coping with Crises.* Leicester: British Psychological Society/Routledge.

Patterson, C. (1986) *Theories of Counselling and Psychotherapy.* New York: Harper and Row.

Pless, I. and Nolan, T. (1991) Revision, replication and neglect in research on maladjustment in chronic illness. *Journal of Child Psychology and Psychiatry, 32,* 347–365.

Pless, I. and Satterwhite, B. (1972) Chronic illness in childhood: Selection, activities and evaluation of non-professional family counselors. *Clinical Pediatrics, 11,* 403–410.

Pruitt, S. and Elliott, C. (1990) Paediatric procedures. In M. Johnston and L. Wallace (Eds) *Stress and Medical Procedures.* Oxford: Oxford University Press.

Rogers, C. (1959) A theory of therapy, personality and interpersonal relationships as developed in the client-centered framework. In S. Koch (Ed.) *Psychology: A Study of a Science.* New York: McGraw-Hill.

Rushton, R. and Davis, H. (1992) An evaluation of training in basic counselling skills. *British Journal of Guidance and Counselling, 20,* 206–221.

Sabbeth, B. and Leventhal, J. (1984) Marital adjustment to chronic childhood illness: a critique of the literature. *Pediatrics, 73,* 762–767.

Sokolov, I. and Hutton, D. (1988) *The Parents Book: Getting on Well with our Children.* Wellingborough: Thorsons.

Stein, R. and Jessop, D. (1984) Does pediatric home care make a difference for children with chronic illness? Findings from the Pediatric Ambulatory Care Study. *Pediatrics, 73,* 845–853.

Swirydczuk, K. (1991) Natalia. In A. Cooper and V. Harpin (Eds) *This is our Child: How Parents Experience the Medical World*. Oxford: Oxford University Press.

Treacher, A. and Carpenter, J. (1984) *Using Family Therapy*. Oxford: Basil Blackwell.

Trower, P., Casey, A. and Dryden, W. (1988) *Cognitive-Behavioural Counselling in Action*. London: Sage.

Wallander, J., Varni, J., Babani, L., Banis, H. and Wilcox, K. (1989) Family resources as resistance factors for psychological maladjustment in chronically ill and handicapped children. *Journal of Pediatric Psychology, 14*, 157–173.

Whitehead, N. (1989) Paediatrics and childhood cancer. In A. Broome (Ed.) *Health Psychology: Processes and Applications*. London: Chapman and Hall.

Worden, W. (1983) *Grief Counselling and Grief Therapy*. London: Tavistock.

Index